Anat Maor

LEGISLATION AND POLITICS

Anat Maor

LEGISLATION AND POLITICS

The Success of Private Legislation in Israel

LAP LAMBERT Academic Publishing

Impressum/Imprint (nur für Deutschland/ only for Germany)

Bibliografische Information der Deutschen Nationalbibliothek: Die Deutsche Nationalbibliothek verzeichnet diese Publikation in der Deutschen Nationalbibliografie; detaillierte bibliografische Daten sind im Internet über http://dnb.d-nb.de abrufbar.

Alle in diesem Buch genannten Marken und Produktnamen unterliegen warenzeichen-, marken- oder patentrechtlichem Schutz bzw. sind Warenzeichen oder eingetragene Warenzeichen der jeweiligen Inhaber. Die Wiedergabe von Marken, Produktnamen, Gebrauchsnamen, Handelsnamen, Warenbezeichnungen u.s.w. in diesem Werk berechtigt auch ohne besondere Kennzeichnung nicht zu der Annahme, dass solche Namen im Sinne der Warenzeichen- und Markenschutzgesetzgebung als frei zu betrachten wären und daher von jedermann benutzt werden dürften.

Coverbild: www.ingimage.com

Verlag: LAP LAMBERT Academic Publishing GmbH & Co. KG
Dudweiler Landstr. 99, 66123 Saarbrücken, Deutschland
Telefon +49 681 3720-310, Telefax +49 681 3720-3109
Email: info@lap-publishing.com

Herstellung in Deutschland:
Schaltungsdienst Lange o.H.G., Berlin
Books on Demand GmbH, Norderstedt
Reha GmbH, Saarbrücken
Amazon Distribution GmbH, Leipzig
ISBN: 978-3-8433-7456-9

Imprint (only for USA, GB)

Bibliographic information published by the Deutsche Nationalbibliothek: The Deutsche Nationalbibliothek lists this publication in the Deutsche Nationalbibliografie; detailed bibliographic data are available in the Internet at http://dnb.d-nb.de.

Any brand names and product names mentioned in this book are subject to trademark, brand or patent protection and are trademarks or registered trademarks of their respective holders. The use of brand names, product names, common names, trade names, product descriptions etc. even without a particular marking in this works is in no way to be construed to mean that such names may be regarded as unrestricted in respect of trademark and brand protection legislation and could thus be used by anyone.

Cover image: www.ingimage.com

Publisher: LAP LAMBERT Academic Publishing GmbH & Co. KG
Dudweiler Landstr. 99, 66123 Saarbrücken, Germany
Phone +49 681 3720-310, Fax +49 681 3720-3109
Email: info@lap-publishing.com

Printed in the U.S.A.
Printed in the U.K. by (see last page)
ISBN: 978-3-8433-7456-9

LEGISLATION AND POLITICS

The Success of Private Legislation in Israel

Dr. Anat Maor

CONTENTS 2

Chapter 1: <u>Introduction and Methodology</u>

> Ladies and gentlemen, there are few previous examples in the history of the   Knesset of a public personality taking up a subject with such firmness and determination, overcoming so many obstacles, and convincing so many people along the way, including myself, and finally achieving the goal of that aspiration, and winning such widespread acclaim.

- remarks by the Speaker of the Knesset, April 19, 1994, after the Second and Third Readings of the Law for the Absorption of Demobilized Soldiers, initiated by MK Raanan Cohen.

In a modern democracy, the act of making laws is of the utmost value because the law is the foundation stone; the law is the supreme authority. Laws, in a democracy, are the outcome of political struggles conducted between parties in the parliament, between the individual Members of Knesset and the government, and between various public interest groups. According to the principle of "separation of powers" proposed by Charles Montesquieu (*On the Spirit of the Laws*, Book I, para. 1), the elected parliament is the legislative authority that is responsible for the drafting and ratification of laws, in addition to their tasks of representing the citizens and supervising the other branches of power; the executive power is responsible for implementation of the laws and for the conduct of the affairs of state and the citizens; and the judicial authority is responsible for decisions relating to deviations from the law.

According to this principle, the primary authority for legislation in a democracy lies in the hands of the parliament. But in a parliamentary regime in which the parliament elects the government from its members, and in which the prime minister and the members of the executive authority are also leaders of their respective political parties, the parties consequently have tremendous political power, and the political power concentrated in the hands of the executive authority is enormous. Mill (1946) argued that representative government presents the national mind, the needs and the qualities of the masses, and the relative strength of different parties and opinions. Other researches also emphasize the growth in governmental power that occurred during recent decades (Andeweg, 1997; B. Doring, 1995; Lowenberg & Patterson, 1979; Olson, 1994).

In fact, what we have seen has been **a role reversal with regard to the initiation of legislation:** the executive authority has assumed the lead role in matters of legislation – an area that rightfully falls within the province of the **legislative authority**, which should bear responsibility for it.

Governments increase their legislative power by two means:

Firstly, the initiative for tabling bills has been concentrated primarily in the hands of governments (the actual initiative for legislation is divided between the legislators and the executive authority). In some countries there are obstacles that impede the tabling of private legislation by MPs. The function of the parliament has become to **ratify** laws rather than to **lead** the legislation.

Secondly, governments have been granted the power to deal with secondary legislation. There are differences between states in regard to the degree to which the executive authority has the power to enact secondary legislation. In Israel, the scope of secondary legislation is wider than that of primary legislation. Thus, the right to initiate legislation is shared in most countries by MPs and the government.

This study will examine legislation that was initiated by individual Knesset members, or private bills. A private bill is a bill initiated by an MK without the initial participation of a government ministry. The research was conducted in the Israeli Parliament (Knesset), but the findings have universal applicability. Many of the phenomena, process, and strategies discussed are familiar in most parliaments. The research pertains to the years 1992-2006. Later this book will examine the origins of parliamentary bills and describe the variety of catalysts that emerge to bring forward the ideas that will be enshrined in the proposed laws.

One very important innovation of this book is the examination of the act of legislation not only as a judicial or procedural process, but as a process of political negotiation. The hypothesis is that private legislation in parliaments is a process of interaction between an MK as private initiator and political actors.

This point of view gives a new perspective to the legislation process. The tools and strategies that Wildavsky (1975; 1964) and Fenno (1973; 1966) used originally to examine the budgeting process in the legislative body are here applied to the process of private legislation.

In the book we will summarize the theories regarding negotiation in general and political negotiation in particular. We will then study the interests and interactions of the central actors in the political arena that take part in the political negotiation of legislation. Then we will present findings on the strategies and tactics used during several legislation processes. The theories and methods of negotiation strategies, which were first rate research tools in the fields of diplomacy, labor relations, and politics, take on a new form in the field of legislation and help us better understand the legislation process as political negotiation.

Another important contribution of this book relates to the perception of the role of the legislator as political initiator in modern parliamentarianism; most of the academic literature relates to the MP as a 'team player' of his faction and party. The conception and findings relating to the role of the legislator as initiator of bills and negotiator with the government significantly expands awareness and perspective on legislation as a political negotiation process.

The Methodology of the Research

The research is **qualitative.** We used four kinds of methodological tools:

1) **Analysis of the qualitative content of primary and secondary sources**, such as:

    a.   The laws that were passed

    b.   Minutes of debates in the Knesset plenary;

    c.   Minutes of sessions of parliamentary committees

    d.   The official resolutions of the Ministerial Committee on Legislative Affairs

    e.   Government decisions (relating to the laws)

    f.   Judgments of the High Court of Justice that pertain to those laws

    g.   Background material that was presented and tabled before the committee

    h.   Official correspondence with the chairman of the committee

    i.   Conclusions and resolutions of the committee

    j.   Documents of the research center of the Knesset

    k.   Research papers/documents/works of research institutes

    l.   Academic or public seminars

    m.   The press.

All these sources have been used and processed in the analysis of qualitative content, and cross-referenced with the theoretical material.

2) **Case studies.** "Case studies" refers to qualitative follow-up on the detailed proceedings. The advantage of this method is that it includes reflections on the events in the contexts and locations in which they took place; thus, it can generate comprehensive descriptive information, providing new insights into the phenomenon being examined (Kenny & Grotkiusheng, 1984). Given the nature of the questions studied, an 'intrusive' kind of methodology was needed (Stake, 1978). The work was based on an in-depth examination of the three case studies, and secondary examination of other laws enacted, inasmuch as this was required:

    a.   The Absorption of Former Soldiers Law (1994); initiated by MK Raanan Cohen of the Labor Party (coalition).

    b.   The Prevention of Sexual Harassment Law (1998); initiated by MK Yael Dayan of the Labor Party (coalition).

    c.   The National Insurance Act (Amendment No. 41 - aid for large families) (2000); initiated by MK Shmuel Halpert of United Torah Judaism (UTJ) (Opposition).

The reasons for choosing these particular laws was their **centrality:** each law concerns either a structural change or a pivotal issue in Israeli society and affects a large segment of the population; the budgetary cost of implementation of each law is high; and the law has aroused widespread repercussions among the public and the media due both to the great interest in it and the controversy it has provoked.

3) **Interview research tool**: the interview gives us the individual, personal, or informal aspect of public policy formation and allows us to see the answers as a personal viewpoint and not only as response and reaction to questions in a questionnaire. The interview allows the researcher to reach emotional and personal dimensions (Zabar Ben Yehoshua, 1995; Shkedi, 2004). Through these research methods, reference is made to other in-depth works of research in the endeavor to illuminate the different phases of policy formation, decision-making, application, and evaluation (Fenno, 1966, 1973; Wildavsky, 1966, 1975). Interviews were conducted with MKs who initiated the legislation and others who were found to have a record (statistically) of active involvement in previous legislation, former justice ministers, and representatives of interest groups.

4) **Participating observation**. This methodology is based on use of quantitative research methods in studies of the House of Representatives, as was done for example by the following three scholars: Fenno (1966), Putnam (1973, 1978), and Wildavsky (1978). They applied the quantitative research method of interviews and participating observation in their comprehensive research into the US Congress, particularly in its method of budgeting and the function of its committees. Fenno (1978) describes the method as one in which the researcher "hangs" about and seeks out the process of interaction, influence, inter-personal relations, power-play, trust or distrust, etc. – like a hunter stalking his prey; Fenno recorded the information, reactions, and his own impressions immediately after his conversations. He calls this method of observation and getting impressions the "over-the-shoulder" method.

The fact that the researcher has herself been a Knesset Member offers many advantages: in regard to her ability to discern the dynamics and rhetoric of debate, to trace informal contacts between the Knesset and the government, to discern who are the leading individuals, and more. There is of course a certain danger of lack of objectivity and over-involvement; consequently this knowledge was nowhere used as the sole source, but only as corroborating evidence. The research does not relate to or analyze any of the laws in the enactment of which the researcher herself was involved, and she has maintained strict objectivity of her research position.

Chapter 2: The Dramatic Growth of Private Legislation in Israel, 1992- 2006

The right to initiate legislation in Israel is shared by the MKs and the government, but a study of the data shows that, throughout most of the terms of office of the Knesset, it was the government that played the major role in initiating legislation (Statistical Summaries on the 1st to 16th Knesset); during the First and Second Knesset (1949-1955), private legislation accounted for only 2% of the laws that were passed; from the Third to the Seventh Knesset (1955-1974)—for 7 to 12%; and during the Eighth to Twelfth Knesset (1974-1988)—for 15 to 24%. Only in the Twelfth Knesset (1988-1992) was there a significant departure from that statistic, and laws arising out of private legislation accounted for 40% of the laws passed. From the Thirteenth to the Sixteenth Knesset (1992-2006), MKs increasingly took into their own hands the initiative for legislation, and laws that **were passed** as a result of private members' legislation initiative account for a greater proportion of the laws passed than those initiated by government.

The hegemony of the collectivist legislation of the government was broken. The following table presents the date (Table 1 & Chart 1):

Stage	Knesset number	Office		Total number of laws passed	Laws initiated by Knesset members		Laws initiated by Knesset committees		Laws initiated by government	
		Start date	End		No.	%	No.	%	No.	%
A	1	1949	1951	218	4	2%	14	6%	200	92%
	2	1951	1955	280	5	2%	1	0%	274	98%
B	3	1955	1959	288	22	8%	2	1%	264	92%
	4	1959	1961	123	12	10%		0%	111	90%
	5	1961	1965	281	34	12%	3	1%	244	87%
	6	1965	1969	260	25	10%	1	0%	234	90%
	7	1969	1974	322	40	12%	3	1%	279	87%
C	8	1974	1977	360	72	20%	0	0%	288	80%
	9	1977	1981	387	81	21%	2	1%	304	79%
	10	1981	1984	200	30	15%	14	7%	156	78%
	11	1984	1988	292	71	24%	2	1%	219	75%
D	12	1988	1992	351	143	41%	0	0%	208	59%

	13	1992	1996	486	250	51%	18	4%	218	45%
E	14	1996	1999	290	138	48%	19	7%	133	46%
	15	1999	2003	463	235	51%	38	8%	190	41%
	16	2003	2006	425	199	47%	17	4%	209	49%
	Total			**5026**	**1361**	**27%**	**134**	**4%**	**3531**	**69%**

*The average percentage of "private legislation" by stage: A - 2%, B - ~10%, C - ~20%, D - ~40%, E - ~50%

*Source: Knesset archives, years 1949-2006

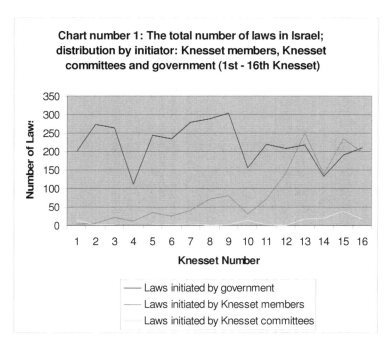

We went on to carry out a comparative study of private member legislation initiating processes in other parliaments.

Below are the comparative data, by percentage, of successful laws initiated privately by Knesset members in relation to the successful laws initiated by the government.[1]

Table 2: Comparisons of legislative success in different countries based on initiative (private, government or other), 2003*

Country	Initiative			Total
	Private	Government	Other	
Israel	51%	43%	6% (Committees)	100%
Italy	35%	64%	1% (Public)	100%
England	29%	71%	-	100%
Germany	26%	69%	5% (Parties)	100%
France	12%	88%	-	100%

* In some of the countries, the statistical data are based on a full year (2003); in others, they are based on the working year of the given parliament (2002-2003). In Israel, because of the fact that 2003 was an election year, the data come from the year 2002.

The comparative study shows that in most parliamentary regimes, there are at least two channels of legislative initiative: government initiatives and private initiatives by MPs. Furthermore, in some countries there are other, less central channels, the source of power being inner parliamentary systems that allow for the tabling of draft bills, parliamentary committees, and in one case public initiative. We chose to study countries which have a parliamentary regime similar to that of Israel. The data indicates that in the major parliaments of Europe, the principal channel for initiation of laws is the government. However, in 2003, legislation initiated by private MPs constitutes a not insignificant proportion of all legislation: in Italy, more than one-third of legislation was initiated by members of parliament (35%); in the UK and Germany, it accounted for **more than one quarter** of legislation (29% in the UK and 26% in Germany). In France the percentage was lower, though even there it accounted for 12% of legislation.   It was thus found that private members' initiative in legislation is common to the parliaments of Europe, but the percentage of such legislation in Israel in the decade from 1992-2003 was higher than in the European parliaments studied.

---

[1] These data come from, respectively: Israel—*Statistical Annual of the Knesset* and Knesset Archives; England—Factsheet L2, Legislation Series, Private Members' Bills Procedure, Revised, November 2004; Germany—Legislate, 02initleg.html, Deutscher Bundestag, Initiation of Legislation; Italy—Rapporto 2004-2005, Sullo stato della Legislazione, in Camera.it files/servizi_cittadini/Rapporto-2004; France—Wright V. (1996), *The Government and Politics of France, Great Britain*, Routledge, pp. 136-142. Some of the data have been updated based on information from the Internet and from the comparative research above. In comparing the data, we have used the study: Rapporto 2004-2005, Sullo stato della Legislazione.

Given such a remarkable increase in legislation initiated privately by Israeli MKs that passed into law, the question examined in the research is: **To what factors can one attribute the significant increase in private members' legislation in Israel from 1992 to 2006?**

Theoretical literature, hypotheses, and the findings of the research

There are three categories of explanatory factors that we examined:

A. **Macro-political changes**, which were taken as the **basic factors** of the research.

B. **Explanatory factors** that we examined in our research, regarding the values and interests of the MK.

C. **Explanatory factors** based on legislation as a **process of political negotiation**

A. Macro-political changes (hypotheses 1-3)

The three macro-political-cultural elements that explain the significant increase in the number of privately initiated laws passed in Israel from 1992-2003 are:

1. The result of changes in perception of the MP on the part of parliaments and in some research: there are those who perceive the role of the MP in the modern era not merely to ratify and approve legislation, to represent and supervise, but also **to play an active role as a political initiator and participant in policy formation.** The scholarly literature shows a decline in the importance of the parliament on the one hand and a transition to its becoming a more active participant in policy formation on the other (Andeweg, 1997; B. Doring, 1995; Lowenberg & Patterson, 1979; Olson, 1994). The changes in the role of parliament have also brought about changes in the choices made by elected MPs in regard to the kind of activity they will engage in; in addition to the aims of political survival and re-election (Fenno, 1996), we must also add motives of political belief (Putnam 1973)—participation in policy formation has given rise to a conception of the individual MP as a political initiator.

However, academic literature tends to view MPs as "group players." The theoretical contribution of the present research is a hypothesis that suggests a new perspective, regarding MPs as **independent political players who become political initiators.** In this light we will examine the characteristics and traits inherent in such political entrepreneurship (initiative) starting with Max Weber (1904), through economic initiatives, and leading up to political initiatives (Doron & Sened 2001). Doron and Sened, in their research, highlighted the concept of legislation initiative as a factor mediating between the public and the decision-makers. This research will focus on the MK as political initiator, on the act of initiating legislation, and on MKs playing an unprecedented role—that of legislation initiator—which had been virtually the sole province of the government and the hegemony of parties.

The following macro-political and cultural factors – relating to developments in Israel during the 1990s – reinforced the notion of the MK and legislator as political initiator.

2. The second macro-political/cultural explanatory factor holds that, with the ideological-normative changes that occurred in Israel during the transition to an **"open society,"** increasing importance was attributed to **individual action and initiative in every sphere of life**. Implications of the normative social, economic, civic, and communications aspects of society also affected the parliamentary arena (Doron & Lebel, 1992). To this should be added other far-reaching changes during the 1990s, such as developments in gender perception and increasing equality between genders (Herzog, 2000; Yezraeli, 2000); the transition from a strong security-slanted perception (Barzilai, 1992; Simon, 2003; Shapira, A. 2004) to a diplomatic perception and the promotion of measures towards peace (Dromi, 2003, 2004); the universality of higher education and the large-scale immigration from the former Soviet Union; all these factors impacted on cultural-political changes in Israel, which placed the greatest emphasis on individual initiatives. In the State of Israel, in which the collectivist concept had for so long held centre stage (Diskin, 1988; Koren, 1999; Shapira, Y. 1975), these were dramatic changes indeed.

3. The third macro-political and cultural explanatory factor relates to changes in the **reciprocal relations between the different authorities in Israel during the 1990s**. While changes in the balance between the various authorities developed gradually, from the moment the executive power began to make sweeping use of the Economic Arrangements Law regarding economic matters and the judicial authority increased its power, MKs also strove to intensify their activity as initiating legislators. The Economic Arrangements Law significantly undermines the powers of the Knesset (Nahmias & Klein, 1999; Adv. Zvi Inbar, December 31, 1998, Adv. Anna Schneider, January 30, 2001 – the legal counselors to the Knesset). Several organizations and associations lodged appeals against this defective legislative procedure, and Supreme Court Justices Barak, Cheshin, and Beinisch actually ruled in one of their judgments that this law was problematic in terms of the democratic process; that the apparatus of the Economic Arrangements Law was being exploited by the government in such a way as to preclude effective parliamentary criticism of the measures it was enacting; and that it was liable to undermine the delicate balance between the executive power and the legislative power (High Court of Justice ruling 4019/03; September 2004). The other 'delicate balance' that was being undermined was that relating to judicial power, specifically increased judicial activism (Mautner, 1993; Segal, 2000; Shitrit, 2004). From the time of the enactment of the Basic Law: Human Rights in 1992, the Supreme Court had assumed the authority of judicial control over legislation, thus spurring MKs to increase the volume of their legislative activity.

This research, which seeks explanations for the dramatic increase in private legislation by MKs from 1992-2006, is based on the hypothesis that the macro-political and cultural changes described above impacted on the type and degree of activity of the individual MK; on developments in the role of parliament and the increased role of the political initiator; on the normative-ideological changes that took place in Israel during the transition to an "open society" during the 1990s and the importance attributed to individual activity; and that the changes that came about in the balance of power between the various echelons of authority served to intensify the trend for individual MKs to initiate legislation, which in turn influenced policy formation.

Let now examine the explanatory factors for the intensified activity of MKs as initiators of legislation.

B. Explanatory factors: values and interests of the MK (hypotheses 4 -5)

The first set of explanations emanates from the **value-based and political considerations and motives of MKs;** ideological considerations on the one hand and the need for political survival on the other.

4. **The values and ideology of the legislator**, which are the source of the ideas behind the initiation of the laws, influences the value-judgment based dimension of the laws and norms of the state, the formation of its policies, and determination of its agenda (Kingdon, 1995; Stone, 1989; Derry, 1997). Researchers who have in recent years drawn increased attention, in their analyses of public policies, to the attitude which stresses the influence of ideas on policy (Influence of Ideas – Surel, 2001; Hansen et al., 2000), assume that ideas have decisive influence on the considerations, analyses, and political decisions behind policy formation, even though economic considerations and interest groups play so important a part in the overall considerations. Putnam (1973) argues that most studies of political structure are based on an analysis of the factors that push and pull the decision-makers, on environmental explanations, and on the analysis of the role and power of parties, interest groups, constituencies, status, and social structure. He does not rule out these factors or belittle their importance, but in his opinion it omits the analysis of the worldview, philosophy, and basic axioms that impact on the personality, orientation, and political behavior of the individuals who deal in politics and policy formation. All these form the infrastructure of the political culture of the decision-makers, which is composed of three factors: their cognitive predispositions, their operative ideals, and their political belief system.

The findings show that **this hypothesis has been confirmed:** MKs who succeeded in their private legislation initiatives were those who initiated **laws based on ideological values,** who had pinpointed problems to which the new legislation provided solutions, on important issues which were of interest to the public, meeting the needs and interests of population groups that were large or that enjoyed great political power.

The sparse research literature that exists so far on the activities of individual MKs mainly stresses motives emanating from the need for re-election (Blander & Klein, 2002; Nahmias, 1999). The present study, however, presents findings that indicate the centrality of the ideological, value-based dimension for the individual legislator.

5. **The next explanation examined relates to the political motives of MKs as they work toward their principal goal, i.e., re-election**. The scholarly literature maintains that the transition to preliminary elections within each political party (primaries), which was introduced in 1992, directly influences the increase in legislation that arose out of initiatives taken by MKs. The direct result of the introduction of primaries has been the emergence of a new code of behavior between the elected MP and the voters, and a decline in the status of the parties (Key, 1976; Frank Soraue, 1964; Scott and Hrebenar, 1979). This has also impacted on the behavior patterns in the Knesset itself, the principal victim of which has been the political party. The party leaders who, until that time, were used to exercising control over the selection of the party's candidates for the Knesset, were now sidelined by politicians who appealed directly to their voting public, sometimes to a very specific voting public (Bar, 1996; Doron, 1996; Hazan, 1999).

At the level of the individual MK, candidates elected by direct vote, in primaries, owe their loyalty to their voters; now they had to stand out and make themselves known and identified by the party's voters, upon whose support they were dependent for their re-election (Fenno, 1966, 1973; Mayhew, 1974; Baram, 1996; Begin, 1996; Doron, 1996).

This hypothesis of the research therefore was that the changes in the method of preliminary selection in the major parties with the transition to the primary system reinforced the behavior pattern of soloist activity by the individual MK, with re-election as the principal aim.

The findings show that this research hypothesis has not been borne out. It was shown in the research that there is no empirical correlation between the number of laws that the MK initiated and got enacted and the duration of his term in the Knesset, nor was there found to be any significant intensification of legislative activity leading up to the primaries. In other words, the second hypothesis has not been proven, and it has been found that there is no correlation between the promotion of legislation and re-election. This finding is compatible with the complexity of "the logic of political survival" as described by Buino de Mystica and others (2003); it remains a basic mystery of politics that, in many cases, leaders who brought peace and prosperity to their respective countries are thrown out of office after being in office for a relatively short period, while leaders who have caused crises, wars, and decline tend to stay at the helm for long periods. The researchers ironically point out that, if they were asked to provide a succinct and catchy headline for their research, it would be "When bad policy is good politics and good policy is bad politics" (p. 12).

However, the findings show that the transition to the primaries system has caused an increase in soloist legislation initiatives on the part of MKs; there appears to be a factual connection between the number of laws tabled in the Knesset and the start date of party primaries (1992). MKs apparently thought the process of legislation would help them win re-election.

C. Explanatory factors based on the process of political negotiation (hypotheses 6-8)

In the other area of the research (hypotheses 6-8), the process of legislation is examined as **a process of political negotiation**, and not only as a legal and procedural process. The mode of conducting negotiations is analyzed by the specialized criteria for the strategy and tactics of conducting political negotiations. Prior research has dealt mainly with the legal and procedural aspects of legislation (Barak, 2004; Inbar, 1993; Rubinstein and Medina, 2005). The present research has made an important contribution by relating to legislative procedure as political negotiation, while examining negotiation strategies and tactics employed to advance the legislation.

Since private legislation is a process of power relations and reciprocal relations between the individual initiating MK and the government, the theoretical approach to it emerges out of theories relating to negotiations and political negotiation. Negotiations are an exchange of words and/or goods, a process of give and take, between two or more people. The aspiration of negotiation is to reach agreement, but that is not an essential condition (Brams and Alan, 1996; Milgrom, 1990; Stevans, 1963; Galin, 1996, 2005).

6. The professional political negotiation skills of the MK[2]

Schelling distinguishes between two categories of negotiation: a. negotiations from which both sides are going to emerge with some benefit (mutually profitable adjustment); and b. negotiations in which one side benefits at the expense of the other. The latter situation involves an element of pure bargaining, since each side is motivated by the knowledge that he will be either the winner or the loser. Galin (2005) categorizes the first type under the traditional school known as "cooperation" and the second overall category is classified under the school of "struggle."

Galin (1996) notes that "the process of negotiation is composed of several stages: first the stage of preparation; then the stage of presenting and justifying the purposes of the negotiation; then the phase of bargaining, which includes proposals and counter-proposals in the presentation of which various tactics are used; and then the final stage in which the preferred alternatives are chosen, summaries are drawn up, and agreement is reached." (p.30)

In this chapter, strategies and tactics used in the course of negotiation are described (Galin, 1996; Milgrom, 1990; Stevans, 1963).

Doron and Sened (2001) developed the theme of **political** negotiation. They claim that in a democratic regime, the most important characteristic of politics is the negotiation process at all its levels: between government and citizens, between government and any other groups and interests in society, between parties and their supporters, etc.

A great deal of research has been conducted on the reciprocal relationship between parliament and government, including the comprehensive research into the process of budget-formation by the US

---

[2] See *supra* chapter 7.

House of Representatives as a process of political negotiation (Fenno, 1966, 1973; Wildavsky 1966, 1975).

The present research examined private legislation as a process of negotiation and power relations between the initiating individual MK and the government, a process in which interest groups play a central role.

The turning-point in the history of privately initiated legislation in the Israeli Knesset occurred in the 12th Knesset, in 1992. The breakthrough came when three initiating MKs succeeded in getting three very significant laws enacted: Basic Law: Human Dignity and Liberty, Basic Law: Freedom of Occupation, and Basic Law: The Government (which provided for direct election of the Prime Minister) (Bachor, 1996; Gavison, 1993; Karp, 1993; Medini, 2004). The influence of these laws has been considerable, not only because of their inherent importance, but also due to the strategies and tactics used in achieving the legislation.

The findings show that **the sixth research hypothesis has been borne out:** the MKs who succeeded in promoting private legislation achieved this by dint of **professionalism, skill, strategies, and tactics used in conducting political negotiation for legislation.**

7. Creating coalitions with extra-parliamentary interest groups[3]

In examining the role of the second political player, we have applied the theory of "Policy Networks," which deals with the formulation of public policy through interaction and mutual relations between civil servants (the institutional approach) and voluntary interest groups (the third sector). The policy network approach suggests an explanation of the manner in which participants in the network cope with or exercise pressure for changing policies or for abiding by existing policies (Menahem, 1999). We shall discuss the importance and manner of action of the interest groups (Anderson C.W, 1979; Norton & Wood, 1990; Norton, 1999; Rothenberg, 11992; Sabatier and Jenkins 1993; Smith, 1995; Yishai, 1997).

The findings show that **the seventh research hypothesis has been borne out:** MKs who succeeded in getting significant laws enacted had succeeded in organizing or putting together an extra-parliamentary coalition of interest groups. The help and support of such interest groups were significant factors in the promotion of private legislation initiatives.

8. The political negotiations of the government.

The third political player who confronts the MK during political negotiations over legislation is of course the government. The Paradigms Policy theory establishes that the system has difficulty adapting to change and with openness to new ideas (Hall, 1993; Howlett and Ramesh, 1995; Menahem, 1999). Hall maintains that, by its very nature, the state favors stability, and consequently political players and the civil service implement only marginal incremental changes. In Israel it was the government that had

---

[3] See *supra* chapter 8.

to adapt to rapid change – to the changed perception of the MKs themselves of their role in the political game – perceiving of themselves as political initiators; it further had to adapt to the change in the behavior patterns of MKs, which stemmed from the introduction of party primaries (beginning in 1992), that directly influenced the MK's attitudes about political survival. However, the government conducts political negotiations on private legislation out of concern for its own interests, and in terms of the new system of checks and balances in the power relations between itself and MKs.

The findings indicate that **the eighth research hypothesis has been borne out;** the success of certain MKs in successfully getting significant laws enacted, and the government's positive response to a substantial proportion of the legislation initiatives taken by MKs, reflects that it has learned to comply with the new rules of the game and that it has come to realize that they actually serve the interests of the government (such as ensuring that members of the coalition abide by their promises of loyalty and reducing the adversarial activities of members of the opposition). For this reason, the government acquiesced to this breakthrough in legislation procedures as long as it did not endanger its own stability or its hold on the reins of power. However, where the government perceived that an act of private legislation was liable to undermine its hold on power, it quickly acted to curb such initiatives (in 2002). That is the subject for a different study.

Conclusions and Contributions of the Present Study

The present study is the first comprehensive study of the dramatic changes that have taken place in the source of legislation in Israel: from the unchallenged role of the government in initiating legislation during the period of the first twelve parliaments in the state of Israel (from 1949-1992), to Knesset Members assuming the leading role in this respect from 1992-2006. Very little research has thus far been conducted into the functioning of the Knesset in general, and into private members' legislation in particular. This fact is particularly perturbing when one considers the extensive research literature that exists on Israel's legal system and the judgments of its courts. The present research should contribute to academic study of the following aspects:

1. **Theoretical contribution to the perception of the role of the legislator as political initiator in modern parliamentarianism.** Most of the research literature relates to the MK as a "team player" of his faction and his party. The conception and findings on the role of the legislator as independent political initiator and as responsible for policy formation build up to an important theoretical perspective.

2. **Study of the ideological motivation of the individual MK (and not only of the political parties) concomitant with motive of re-election.** Previous research into private legislation initiatives in Israel has focused primarily on the MK's motivation to seek re-election, the budgetary aspect, and the way in which such initiatives clash with the institution of government.

16

The present research concentrates more on the centrality of the ideological and value-based component of the motives for legislative initiatives.

3. **Theoretical contribution to the analysis of legislative processes such as political negotiations (not only from the legal, procedural, and budgetary perspectives).** The research will contribute to characterizing and discerning the way decisions on legislation are made, such as political negotiations between MKs and the government, with the involvement of various interest groups. A contribution similar to the strategic and tactical analysis made by Wildavsky (1966, 1975) and Fenno (1966, 1973) in regard to budgetary procedures of the US House of Representatives is made by the present research vis-à-vis private legislation in Israel, using the theories and methods of negotiation strategy which were the prime tool of research in the field of political negotiation. Theories relating to labor relations between employer and employees contributed to an innovative understanding of the legislation process as a process of political negotiation between the initiating MK and the government, with the support of extra-parliamentary mediators.

4. **Innovative research into the comparative perspective of private legislation.** In the study comparing private legislation in Israel with that in several European parliaments, emphasis was placed on comparison between the laws that were passed, based on the assumption that the significant data relate to the draft bills actually passed into law (and not the number of draft bills that were tabled). The analysis of this aspect revealed that in the European parliaments studied as well, the percentage of legislation initiated by private Members of Parliament is far from negligible, fluctuating between just over 10%-35% of all legislation passed.

Chapter 3: <u>The Conceptual Sources for Initiating Private Legislation</u>

The first stage in the legislative process is the stage of initiation. This is the most central stage, which influences the values-based dimension of the array of the laws and norms of the country, shapes policy and sets the public agenda (Kingdon, 1995; Stone, 1989; Derry ,1999). Kingdon argues that this stage, the process of setting the public agenda, is extremely important in the shaping of public policy; nevertheless, because it is difficult to define its characteristics, they have not been adequately stressed in public-policy research. The question is: how can this topic be placed on the public agenda? How can we pinpoint when an idea's time has come? When we talk about setting the agenda, there is great significance to defining these problems and their characteristics.

The process of defining the problem is not merely semantic, but political. In order to deal with the raising (or dropping) of an issue or problem on the public agenda, it is essential to highlight and emphasize the worldviews which stand behind their definitions. A "problem" is not a statistical situation or fact, but a dynamic state, and therefore one must identify and uncover its definitions, including bringing to the surface its hidden aspects—instead of focusing merely on the obvious ones. The nature of the problem is expressed in the level of its seriousness, its frequency or infrequency, the continuity or discontinuity of its appearance, one's proximity to or distance from the site of its occurrence. Similarly, we must distinguish between cases in which raising issues on the agenda is the fruit of premeditation and cases of a circumstantial nature. The definition of the problem will differ based on the positions of the different players: the politicians, the community of experts, the public—and within it, the various interest groups (Derry, 1997).

The lone MK or group of MKs is the one who present and advance private bills. However, the reservoir of inspiration and the source for these private bills is extremely varied.

From studies of this phenomenon, from interviews with MKs, and from a painstaking analysis of private social legislation in the Knesset in the years 1992-2003, we may derive the facts of this extensive values-based social legislation. The inspirations for and the sources of this legislation are varied and motivated by the public interest at their most basic level.

1.   Personal initiative of an MK based on worldview and priorities

All of the interviewed MKs noted that the primary inspiration and conceptual impetus for the bills they propose is their worldview: the issues they dealt with before being elected to Knesset, their areas of expertise, and the information they already knew (this category includes some of the laws which were presented in the context of the entire party).

Prominent examples of socially progressive legislation, in the private initiatives of members of the 13th, 14th and 15th Knessets, include: the Council for Higher Education Law (Amendment #10), 1995 (establishing the academic colleges, which provided a breakthrough in the decentralization of higher education); the Senior Citizens Law (Amendment #3), 1996, 1998 (giving pensioners discounts for cultural events, transportation, and medication; this is also the amendment forcing municipalities to give discounts to pensioners on their property taxes); the Minimum Wage Law (Amendment #2), 1997 (raising the minimum wage in part and strengthening methods of enforcement); the Rehabilitation of the Mentally Handicapped in the Community Law, 2000; the Social Security Law (Amendment #59), 2002 (providing for a more just distribution of social security taxes).

These laws, along with many others, are examples of legislation that is values-based and ideological—not merely sectoral.[4]

2. *Completing the work of previous MKs*

Many laws are the fruit of the initiatives of MKs from previous tenures who had not succeeded in passing their bills before they either became ministers or completes their terms. In this case, the bills may be transferred, like a runner's baton in a relay race, to the legislators currently serving (generally from the same party, or at least having a worldview similar to that of the initiators).

There are many examples of progressive private legislation originally proposed in the 13th, 14th or 15th Knessets but passed later. Both the Basic Law: Human Dignity and Liberty and the Basic Law: Freedom of Occupation are based on private members' bills. The Basic Law: Bill of Basic Human Rights, 1963 was initiated by Member of Knesset Yitzhak Klinghoffer (General Liberals-Gachal). Similarly, the Compulsory Education Law (Amendment #16), providing free education from age 3, passed in 1996, but it was based on a 1984 law addressing the same issue, which was voided by the Economic Arrangements Law of 1985. In addition, the Sexual Harassment Prevention Law (Amendment #2), 2004, which recognized the power imbalance in the lecturer-student relationship, was a private member's bill already in 1999.[5]

---

[4] For a comprehensive list of the essential laws that arose from MKs' private initiatives, see Appendix 10.
[5] In addition to laws that were finally passed after many years, the MKs interviewed cited many examples of bills which are legacies, inherited by each Knesset but not yet actually passed. This list includes: the proposed Basic Law: Social and Economic Rights; the proposed Basic Law: Legislation; the proposed Basic Law: Freedom of Expression and Association; the proposed Abortions for Social Reasons Amendment of the Criminal Penalties Law; the Civil Marriage and Divorce Bill; the Compulsory Pension Bill (coming up since 1995, after the adoption of the Compulsory Health Insurance Law); the Wage Limits for Public Service Bill; the Labor Settlement Bill (anchoring farmers' rights to their land); the Tax Deduction for Childrearing Costs Bill (making childrearing costs a recognized expense); the Compensation for Evacuees of Judea, Samaria, the Gaza Strip and the Golan Heights Bill; and the Organ Donation Encouragement Bill.

3. Initiatives of institutional organizations

Many times, legislation is initiated in the reverse manner, i.e., from the grassroots: motivated organizations, non-profits or institutions promote issues that seem important to them and which they do not anticipate being able to raise via the government; they bring the idea or even the text of the bill to MKs, so that the legislators will advance them.[6] The MKs interviewed noted that they saw part of their role being to advance the laws of organizations which represent issues reflecting their ideological values.

The network of these initiatives for legislation is fed by varied organizations and is spread over many spheres:

Promoting workers' issues (using the legislative impetus of the Histadrut): Government Service Law (Pension, Amendment #38) 1997 (removing a bureaucratic hurdle for retired teachers' pensions); Work and Rest Hours Law (Amendment #8), 1993 (adjustment of the 45-hour workweek); Manpower Contractors Law (requiring workers' being included in the collective agreement after nine months).

Promoting women's issues (using the legislative impetus of women's organizations): Women's Labor Law (Amendment #14), 1997 (strengthening the struggle against the unlawful termination of pregnant women); Equal Opportunity in Employment Law (Amendment #3), 1995 (expansion and providing law-enforcement tools); Criminal Penalties Law (Amendment #3), 2001 (criminalizing threatening harassment).

Promoting the needs of single-parent families (using the legislative impetus of single-parent advocacy organizations): Income Security Law (Amendment #12), 1998 (extending child allowance to single-parent families); Single-Parent Families Law (Amendment), 1994 (recognizing *agunot*—women chained by their husbands' refusal to grant a divorce—as single parents).

Protecting women from violence (using women's organization and sexual assault victims' centers): Single-Parent Families Law (Amendment), 2001 (single-parent rights for women in

---

[6] There is yet to be a study analyzing the scope of the growth of legislative initiatives by extra-parliamentary organizations and the distribution of these initiatives between the government and the MKs. However, this study attests to the great number of bills brought to MKs by extra-parliamentary organizations. Similarly, a number of central extra-parliamentary organizations founded, in the 1980s and 1990s, departments of their own to deal with legislative initiatives, from the government and from private members, and accompany the legislation through the Knesset. The Association for Civil Rights in Israel, founded in the 1970s, has contributed to the strengthening of the legislative orientation of extra-parliamentary organizations, in tandem with government legislation. Similarly, the Israel Women's Network, founded in 1987, was the first women's organization to put an emphasis on legislative initiatives and work hard with MKs. In addition, in 1992, the Knesset first established the Lobby for Children and Youth at Risk; the Israel National Council for the Child and other organizations dedicated to the advancement of children's issues directed many bills toward it, paralleling their work with the government itself.

shelters); Criminal Penalties Law (Amendment #47), 1996 (extending the statue of limitations for sexual offenses).

Promoting the needs of children (using the legislative impetus of the Israel National Council for the Child and other organizations dedicated to children's issues): Torts Ordinance (Amendment #9), 2000 (banning striking children); Tax Ordinance Prohibition Act (Collection) (Amendment #4), 2000 (prohibiting confiscation of property in the presence of a child); National Service Bill (conditions of service for those who volunteer for a year of service in a youth movement). The bill was proposed in 1999, but this issue was resolved with regulations.

Advancing the needs of Holocaust victims (using the initiative of organizations for victims of Nazi persecution): the Invalids (Nazi Persecution) Law (Amendment #11), 2001 (compensation for children in the Holocaust).

Advancing the needs of people with disabilities (using the initiative of different organizations dedicated to advancing the status of people with disabilities): the Equal Rights for People with Disabilities Law, 1998 (at the initiative of the Constitution, Law and Justice Committee); the Relief for the Deaf Law (Amendment), 1995 (closed-captioning for television).

Similarly, grassroots organizations have been pivotal in advancing citizen's needs in the local government, the periphery, the settlements and the frontline communities.

Indeed, there are many other examples of organizations which brought up legislative initiatives to MKs in the years 1992-2003. Analysis of the visions, goals, and agendas of these social organizations testifies to a general values-based social approach, which places legislation at the forefront of public awareness, responding to the social needs of wide segments of the population and/ or weak groups within it, not the advancement of narrow interests or the interests of the powers that be.

4.   *Initiative of non-profits which address single issues*

Another impetus for initiating legislation is the social issues raised by *ad hoc* organizations or organizations which have been set up for one issue and act for its advancement by way of legislation. Sometimes, MKs will identify the issue that these organizations raise as essential and imperative, pointing out the neglect or deprivation of a certain segment of the population, and they will enlist in the struggle to advance these laws.

Examples of this progressive private legislation, having a values-based social aspect raised by *ad hoc* organizations, in the abovementioned Knessets include: at the initiative of Ma'an, the Workers Advice Center (advocating for the economic advancement of women)—the Compulsory Tender Law (Amendment #15), 2002 (preference for businesses run by women); at the initiative of incest victims— the Criminal Penalties Law (Amendment #72), 2002 (a further extension of the statute of limitations for

21

sexual offenses); at the initiative of victims of predatory mortgages—the Mortgagors' Protection Law (Legislative Regulations), 2002; by WePower (Ken—Women's Electoral Power)—the Parties Bill (Amendment: Ensuring Representation of Both Genders), which passed its first reading.

5.   *Personal appeals (from the public)*

Many basic issues, which require legislation to resolve them, are raised by public appeals. Some of them require specific solutions because of bureaucratic roadblocks or the human inattentiveness of those in charge of area in the relevant authority. However, some personal appeals from the public raise issues for which the law has no response; therefore, dealing with the specific problem cannot solve them. These issues require a root treatment of the legislative lacuna concerning the problem. In these cases, the MKs, whose role is essentially public (not to be a substitute for the welfare services), initiate laws responding to the distress of the specific person turning to them and to the general problem as well.

Examples of socially progressive private legislation in the abovementioned Knessets which came into being because of appeals from the public include: the Social Security Law (Amendment #83), 1994 (providing for a full maternity grant, not only 70%); the Severance Pay Law (Amendment #6), 1995 (extending severance pay to independent owners as well); the Government Service Law (classification of party activities and collections of funds) (Amendment #3), 2001 (fixing a situation which prevented teachers, nurses, etc. from taking part in party primaries); the Class Action Law (responding to the traps and misdirection of real-estate marketers, who would ensnare the renters of vacation homes).

6.   *Specific or political events which cause a bill to be proposed*

Another values-based source of is the flow of life itself. Occasionally political or specific events place issues on the public agenda; there is then a need to codify it in legislation. When the government is reluctant to act, MKs initiate and advance bills which respond to the absence of a law on the issue (a lacuna) or injustices in other areas.

One example of private legislation in the abovementioned Knessets inspired by real-life events is the Mandatory Minimum Sentencing Law, legislated because of lenient sentences for the perpetrators of rape and domestic violence. Another example is the Firearms Law (Amendment #12), 1999, limiting weapons rights in dangerous situations. The law entered the legislative pipeline and passed in light of a number of cases of murder in which the killer's occupation provided easy access to a firearm. Similarly, the Antiquities Law (Amendment #3), 2002, protecting antiquities from damage and looting, came into being because of a dramatic increase in the theft of antiquities. Finally, the Local Authorities Law (Legislative Regulations) (Elections Arrangements) (#3), 1998, prohibits voting in local elections by someone who had already voted in a different locality—preventing voter fraud due to fictitious addresses. The law was crafted because of the increase in voter fraud in various elections.

7.   *Inspiration from High Court of Justice rulings*

Another reservoir of values-based issues for legislation or for legislative changes may be found in the rulings of the High Court of Justice or other courts. The rulings of the court are usually specific. The legislator, upon discovering the general social, values-based issue, "translates" it into a bill, and its approval grants it the status of an imperative ruling.

A prominent example of socially progressive private legislation in the abovementioned Knessets which follows a ruling of the High Court of Justice is the law to open combat professions to woman, the Military Service Law (Amendment #11), 2000. To a great extent, it is based on the ruling of the High Court of Justice about Alice Miller, who claimed and won the right to serve as an Israeli Air Force pilot.[7]

Another example of the High Court's ruling which has been a source of inspiration in the issue of retirement age and equal pension rights for men and women is the case of Dr. Naomi Nevo (which precedes by some years the time frame of this study).[8] On the topic of equal division of property among spouses during a divorce, a bill was proposed in the footsteps of the Bavil ruling,[9] but this bill never became law. There were cases in which the Knesset legislation and the ruling of the High Court of Justice emerged in parallel: this is what happened with the Sexual Harassment Law of 1998, as well as the Torts Ordinance (Amendment #9), 2000 (banning striking children).

8.   *Legislation based on public commissions or commissions of experts*

Another basis of values-based issues for private legislation or suggestions to amend the law is the institution of public commissions of inquiry or expert commissions. Thus, for example, the Prevention of Violence in the Family Law, 1991, came about following the conclusions of the Karp Report (Yehudit Karp was Deputy Attorney General in the Ministry of Justice). Similarly, the laws relating to the institution of international adoption sprang from the recommendations of a commission headed by Professor Eliezer Yaffe: the Child Adoption Law (Amendment #2), 1996, and later on, the Social Security Law (Amendment #98), 1995 (giving a maternity grant to adoptive parents as well). The report of the Public Commission to Examine the Status of the Child, headed by Justice Saviona Rotlevi, became a basis for laws relating to the advancement of children; the report on the needs of students with learning disabilities became the basis of a bill to integrate them in the regular education system (the

---

[7] HCJ 94/ 4541 Alice Miller v. Minister of Defense, et al. (*PD* 49, 4, 94).
[8] HCJ 87/ 104 Dr. Naomi Nevo v. National Labor Court, et al. (*PD* 45, 2).
[9] HCJ 92/ 1000 Hava Bavli v. Supreme Rabbinical Court (*PD* 48).

legislation began in the 15th Knesset, but it has not yet passed). Finally, the Sheinin Commission report on road accidents led to a number of legislative initiatives.

9. *Influence of international treaties and comparative legislation*

When it comes to many laws, the MKs rely on examples of comparable international legislation. This was what happened with the law to establish the Authority for the Advancement of the Status of Women within the Prime Minister's Office; the legislation advanced on the issue of affirmative action in Israel, starting in 1993, was based on the affirmative action program pursued in the United States starting with the Civil Rights Act of 1964 and the concept of affirmative action in the European Union. In terms of the rights of the disabled and setting up a committee for disabled persons, the Knesset Constitution, Law, and Justice Committee relied on precedent which has its source in a Canadian law; in setting up a committee for equality in occupation, charged with enforcing labor laws, the MKs proposing it relied on the experience accrued in various European countries.

10. *Other sources of inspiration*

Interviews with MKs reveal that there are other sources which influence the initiations of laws:

Laws that emerge from technological developments address new issues on the public agenda. Some examples of this are the Computer Law, the Genetic Information Law, the laws which limit radiation from cellular telephones, limits on Internet use (pornographic materials, racial incitement, violence)—as well as, on the other hand, the Electronic Signature Law.

Laws that are initiated or advanced with the assistance of academia can be very influential. For example, the testimony of MK Yael Dayan relied on academic assistance in the Sexual Harassment Prevention Law, 1998. (See the chapter on the relationship between MKs and extra-parliamentary actors.)

Laws that are inspired by personal experience have universal applications. The personal experiences of MKs can expose them to some universal problem. This is what happened with MK Meir Sheetrit, who suffered a personal tragedy when his daughter died of cancer. Because of this, he initiated the Sick Pay Law (Amendment #3), 1997, which gives a parent additional vacation days to treat a sick child. (This was expanded in continuing legislative regulations to allow supporting a sick parent; in addition, a bonus of 50% was set aside for single parents).

Finally, there are even laws which are born from budget cuts. The Public Libraries Law (Amendment), 2002, codified the obligations of the State to contribute to the budgets of public libraries. (However, it was voided by the Economic Arrangements Law, 2003).

We have thus found that values and worldview constitute very central elements in the legislative actions of MKs. This position found pronounced expression among all of the interviewed MKs. Analysis of the sources of inspiration for legislation, as we spelled them out above, points to a great and broad variety of the bases of legislation, which represent wide domains and sectors of society and the population, reflecting a world of universal social and economic values and needs.

The MKs who succeeded in private legislative initiatives created values-based, ideological laws. They were wise enough to locate and to initiate laws which responded to important issues, were of great public interest, and answered the needs and interests of varied population groups with changing political power.

Chapter 4: <u>Spirit of the Law: The Values-Based Dimension of Bills</u>

Selecting issues for legislation and the content of bills, whether sponsored by private members or the government, expresses the worldviews and priorities of their initiators. The sources that influence the selection of subjects for legislation are values-based and ideological, expressing the worldview of the legislator and responding to the interests of groups or issues which the legislator wants to advance. The legislator must take into account the practical considerations of the odds of advancing the bill and his ability to build coalitions to make possible its passage into law.

In recent years, researchers have dedicated an increasing amount of attention to analyzing public policy from within, an approach which stresses the influence of ideas on policy (Surel, 2000; Hansen & King, 2000). This approach assumes that ideas have crucial influence on the decisions, considerations, and political analyses—at the same time that economic considerations and interest groups fill an important role in this realm.

The ideological approach stresses the metaphysical values, normative values, and images and conceptions of identity. The scholar Surel claims that, using cognitive and normative perceptions and variables, one may explain the differences in policies, the portability of ideas, and the management of stressful situations and social conflict.

As Patton and Sawicki (1993) put it, the question of basic justice lies at the root of all public policy decisions. According to them, it is insufficient to discuss ethical norms alone. One must expand its basis in order to relate to ethical philosophies of nature and human justice and to discuss every issue of meta-ethics, which deals with levels of epistemology and semantics in the sphere of public policy. Societies, philosophies, and religions have been yearning from time immemorial to answer the question: what is social justice?

The world-renowned expert Robert Putnam (1973), an adviser to U.S. President Clinton, argues that most studies of political structure are based on an analysis of the factors which push and pull the decision-makers; on environmental explanations; on the analysis of the role and power of parties, interest groups, areas of choice, and social status and structure. He does not negate these factors, nor does he minimize their importance or integrality, but according to him what is most consequential is the study of positions, views, and basic assumptions, which influence the character, the orientation, and the behavior of those who involve themselves in politics and shaping policy. All of these constitute the cultural-political infrastructure (of those who make the decisions), which is made up of three levels:

- The first level: the fundamental views that constitute the broadest of worldviews

- The second level: the ideal operative values, which constitute the normative positions

- The third level: the political beliefs relating to the norms of the steps which are being taken

26

Putnam conducted a comparative study of views and positions among British and Italian MPs (1973). He analyzed these elements in a very specific questionnaire, and he reaches the conclusion that political norms and values influence the shaping of policy in a decisive way. According to him, the facts which he gleans support the hypothesis that a large part of the differences between the British Parliament's conduct and the Italian Parliament's conduct is explained by the differences in the basic approaches of politicians to the issues of democracy, political egalitarianism, and liberalism.

The researcher Rokeach (1973) defines a value as a "social product" generated over the course of many years using the institutions of society. He divides values into two types, which themselves can be sorted into subcategories: instrumental values, which include moral values and skills-based values; and terminal values, which include personal values which are egocentric (for example, the desire for personal welfare) and societal values, which are centered on society (for example, the desire for world peace). A "value" expresses a preference of that which is desired by the individual. As for the link between values and behavior, as Rokeach puts it, values have a great weight in directing human activity. The network of values is a learned organization of principles and laws, which bring us to decisions and determinations. Rokeach defined seven characteristics of values which constitute standards of behavior: 1) those which direct us to take a position on issues of welfare; 2) those which direct us to favor initially a political or religious ideology; 3) those which help us represent the ego towards others; 4) those which serve as a metric for judging ourselves and others; 5) those which constitute a central body in a comparative social research; 6) those which constitute a guide for the values of others who can be influenced; 7) those which aid in the process of rationalizing and explaining behavior.

The researchers Barnea and Schwartz (1998) analyze the link between values and voting in Israel, and they have found that there are values which are tied to voting; people vote in accordance with their predispositions, which spring from their values. They argue that values are a factor embodying guiding principles in human life, so that within every value there is a central aim which it serves. There are more than a few cases in which there is a direct link between values and the intent of behavior.

An expert on decision-making, Professor Yehezkel Dror (1989), sets out a critical reference for the influence of values networks upon decision-makers in the political arena. According to him, devotion to different factors, including values, can cause misperceptions of reality, which may greatly influence the decision-making process. He calls this preventative irrationalism.

Values-based selection of issues for legislation: the ideological dimension

Three individual case studies will allow us to analyze the findings on this issue, based on interviews and data that we have collected concerning private legislation. We will point to the sources of initiating legislation, which express the worldview of the initiating legislators and of those who serve as a magnet for legislative ideas.

Analysis of the content of the bills' explanatory sections and the speeches of the MKs who initiated the bills in these three cases shows that the initiators of a law attribute a meaningful values-based worldview to the basic concepts implicit within the law. Sometimes, one may feel in these speeches the blood, sweat, and tears that the MKs poured out in order to craft these bills.

1. *The values-based view of the Absorption of Discharged Soldiers Law*

MK Ra'anan Cohen presented the Absorption of Discharged Soldiers Law as part of a Zionist and social view, articulating the belief that the State of Israel, the national home of the Jewish people, must be responsive to the needs of the young people who grow up in it, and above all, to the needs of discharged soldiers. The values-based view of this he laid out in his speeches in the Knesset plenum, when the law was debated in its preliminary, first, second and third reading. His main arguments were:

- We must put an emphasis on the issue of reintegration and be concerned about the younger generation. On a personal level, he added: "The discharged soldiers are part of us: they are our sons and our daughters; they are our future" (Preliminary Reading, 25.11.92).

- A warning about the danger of emigration; MK Cohen played a number of times in his speeches on this patriotic argument.

- The law responds to and focuses on three integral and agreed-upon goals, each of which is equally important for discharged soldiers: education, employment, and housing.

- MK Cohen stressed the obligation of the state to those who served it and gave it the best years of their lives; according to him, this is the obligation of the state towards the soldiers. Just as they have fulfilled their obligation to the state, so it is upon the state to fulfill its obligations to them.

For this values-based, ideological view, MK Cohen found many partners from the members of the Discharged Soldiers Association—above all, high-ranking retired army officers and authority heads.[10] The head of the association, Major General (ret.) Moshe Nativ, stressed an additional reason, equating the conditions of Israeli youth who have completed their army service and need to be "absorbed" back into civilian life with the conditions and benefits for immigrants. Nativ argued that equalizing these benefits would be just, and the process would also bring an end to the estrangement and antipathy of the Israelis towards new immigrants. This view had also been accepted by the initiator.

If so, in the values-based, ideological dimension, the Absorption of Discharged Soldiers Law is, in the view of the initiator, a social-nationalistic-Zionist law, not a mere welfare law. For this reason, the initiator opposed handing off the implementation of this issue to the Ministry of Labor and Social

---

[10] The Association for Discharged Soldiers was a public council with 31 members, at its head Moshe Nativ, who had been the head of the Manpower Directorate within the Israel Defense Forces. Many of its members were people with a public-service or political background.

Welfare; he consistently argued that issue should be treated as a state-public issue, to be dealt with by the Prime Minister's Office.[11]

Thus, we may see in the ideological viewpoint behind the Absorption of Discharged Soldiers Law a values-based infrastructure. This issue has a wide social scope; the fact is that the State of Israel has conscripted most of its sons and daughters for decades, giving the issue a far-reaching and inclusive dimension.

2.   *The values-based infrastructure of the Sexual Harassment Prevention Law*

In the Sexual Harassment Prevention Law, the first paragraph immediately demonstrates a deep values-based view which defines the point of the law in a broad and far-reaching way: proscribing sexual harassment in order to protect human dignity, liberty, and privacy and in order to advance gender equality.

The initiators of the law, MK Yael Dayan and all of the female MKs, had sought to protect the principle of human dignity and to prevent impinging on it. In other words, the concept of sexual harassment does not only appear as a network of definitions, which comes as an outgrowth of the law, but as a full and complete conception of the status of women.

The Hebrew terminology for sexual harassment, *hatrada minit*, is a literal translation of the concept in English, as it was developed in the 1970's in the United States, mainly by Professor Catharine Alice MacKinnon, a leading feminist of the radical stream (Kamir, 2002).

The definition of sexual harassment as impinging on equality and personal dignity, as undermining the self-esteem of the woman, and as a legal issue which relates to an offense towards women was a great accomplishment for the view of equality of the sexes. For the first time in Israel, women had crafted a legal category which came to protect their rights. This was a cultural, social, and legal revolution of the first order.

The law was particularly important taking account the fact that in Israel, as in many countries, sexual harassment was a common social phenomenon, seen at most as a minor, trivial and harmless annoyance. Men were not aware or conscious of their offense against women, and many times they would relate to this phenomenon as a positive, masculine exercise of camaraderie (Dayan, Ayalon, and others in the Knesset debates, 10.3.98; Kamir 2002).

---

[11] The issue of the body responsible for implementation of the Absorption of Discharged Soldiers Law was so important and symbolic in the eyes of the initiating MK that he was forced to rephrase the law. Rather than pass it with the Ministry of Labor and Social Welfare, the 'natural' address for such concerns, named as the implementing body, MK Cohen rewrote the bill to refer to "the minister whom it concerns". After the legislation, an amendment to the law was passed, making the Minister of Defense responsible for implementing the law (26.7.95).

It turns out that the Sexual Harassment Prevention Law as well has a solid infrastructure of values and culture.[12]

3.   *The Values-Based Foundation of the National Insurance Law—Helping Large Families*

Social justice is a universal value, and according to MK Shmuel Halpert, this is the basic value which stood before him when he initiated the Child Allowances Law:

> The idea for the Child Allowances Law was mine, but I arrived at this idea after the publication of the Poverty Report. Every year the number of children living below the poverty line increases, and it became clear that the essence of poverty is within families blessed with children.

"Families blessed with children" is the euphemistic term for large families in Israel, those with at least three children. Halpert adds that he sees that:

> There is a great danger in the fact that children grow up in poverty and famine. A child who grows up in poverty is irreversible damage to the State. He grows up frustrated. While a child should be happy and care-free, he grows up as at totally different citizen.

MK Halpert rejects the criticisms of the high cost of the law by relying on a framework of values and the proper distribution of resources, according to his values, for the good of the entire state and not just for the benefit of the Ultra-Orthodox population, which he represents. In his words at the plenum speech (28.3.2000, in the first reading), he argued:

> The State of Israel invests a great fortune in the absorption of new immigrants, justifiably. But why is it not prepared to invest in internal immigration as well? Benefits for families blessed with children will encourage in a significant way internal immigration, which is an integral strength of the state. We all know that one million more Jews in the state can cause a revolution in the political, security and economic sphere.

In an interview, he adds:

> Today there are 300,000 children who are literally hungry for bread. I told the Finance Minister from the Knesset podium: thirty years ago, when a girl in Bet She'an would say, 'I'm hungry,' the entire country would be shocked. Now, 300,000 children live below the poverty line, and everyone is silent.[13] They say that the greatest expense is for the first child and the second child, but the opposite is true![14] Therefore, one does not need to give a uniform allowance from the first child, and in all the enlightened countries the child allowances are progressive. The more children there are, the greater the allowance must be.

---

[12] We will expand on the importance of the Sexual Harassment Prevention Law in Chapter 10.

[13] These are the statistics of the National Insurance Institute, as they were presented in a meeting of the Labor and Welfare Committee (26.6.00).

[14] MK Halpert notes in an interview: "As the Deputy Minister of Labor and Welfare in the years 1991-1992, I learnt about national insurance. We will take the costs of a family with two children. There remains for each child sufficient untaxed income. This is what the Insurance says; two children—2000 shekels per child; the second one reaches five children, the untaxed income for each child is 800 shekels, and at eight children, 400 shekels. Therefore, in every enlightened country, child allowances are progressive. For example, the Yitzhak family, our neighbors, returned to France. They could not earn a living. Indeed, in France [the father] is a rabbi, but they told me that they could subsist on the allowances alone."

In addition, MK Halpert indicated in an interview that aside from the socio-political motivation, his personal background constitutes a deep impetus in proposing this legislation (a fact which he revealed only in an interview, not in his plenum speech):

> I tried very hard to pass this law out of the deep realization that it would rescue tens of thousands of children from poverty. As a Holocaust survivor, I was hungry for bread, and I can understand the significance of a starving child... At the time of the Holocaust, I was in Romania. I was a young boy, and I remember the hunger which filled the house. There was simply no bread to eat. My parents survived miraculously. Father was in a labor camp, while Mother struggled with the young children. There were three children. There simply was not anything to eat.

Thus, it is clear from the explanatory sections of the laws and the protocols of the case studies that these three Knesset members give the dimension of values a very central role in proposing legislation. We may say that they see in them the talmudic concept of *tikkun olam*—repairing the world.

Chapter 5: The Process of Private Legislation

The act of crafting legislation is very important in modern democracy, because the law is the supreme authority. Consequently, the framework of laws expresses the totality of society's values, norms, rules of government, prescriptions, and proscriptions.

The rule of law is a basic principle of democracy. The President Emeritus of the Supreme Court, Aharon Barak (2004, pp. 116-122), enumerates three views of this issue:

First is the formal view, according to which all of the actors in the state, be they individuals, associations, or government bodies, must act in accordance with the law, and any deviation from it must be answered with an organized sanction of society. The formal significance, if so, is twofold: the legality of authority and the rule of law. The two of these obligate the legislator himself to honor the law; the judicial authority to act according to the objective rule of law; and the executive authority to recognize the limits placed upon it by the law. The rule of law requires that it be enforced. From the time that the verdict is issued, the executive authority is responsible for its application.

Second is the theoretical view, according to which, in order for the rule of law to last, there is a need to provide the elementary circumstances which allow the rule of justice rather than the rule of human caprice: the law must be universal, known, and publicized; it must be clear and understandable; and it must be stable. Furthermore, the law cannot be applied *ex post facto*; laws cannot be allowed to contradict each other; laws cannot demand the performance of acts which cannot be practically executed; and there must be an appropriate enforcement network of government bodies. The American philosopher John Rawls, one of the greatest philosophers of the 20th century, enumerates the following bases which guarantee the existence of formal justice: First, whatever the law decrees must be possible to execute. Second, the principle of equality must be exacting—only if similar cases receive the same or similar treatment may a person hope to exist in the context of the society. Third, there is no offense without the law. Consequently, the law must be known and public; it is forbidden to enact retroactive legislation; the law must be clear and understandable. Fourth, one must fulfill the dictate of natural justice.

The third approach enumerated by Barak is the characteristic view, which is necessary because the formal view and the theoretical view have nothing to do with the content of the law—in fact, it may in practice be logically feasible to accept corrupt laws. Therefore, the widely-held view is that the formal and theoretical views are too limited, and there is not enough in them to give the rule of law its full expression:

> Totalitarian governments as well conduct themselves according to the laws of their countries, which are the laws which they themselves have instituted for their aims and according to their

plots. For example, the Nazis rose to power legally and committed most of their crimes using the powers of explicit legal authority that they took for themselves for this purpose, yet no one can say that in Nazi Germany there was 'the rule of justice' and no one will dispute that their a criminal government ruled.

(Hayim Cohen, 1991)

A characteristic rule of justice needs "to balance different values, principles and interests of a democratic society, within which the government is authorize to use its judgment, striking a fitting balance between appropriate considerations" (Rivlin, HCJ 1993/ 03, 835).

Legislation Initiated by Private Members, the Government, or Parliamentary Committees

There are three channels of initiation for Knesset legislation: bills which are initiated by members of the house, called "private (members') bills"; bills which are brought to the Knesset at the government's behest, under the title of "government legislation"; and bills which are proposed by the Knesset committees.

Let us examine the characteristics of each of these three categories.

Bills initiated by private members of Knesset—proposing a bill is a right reserved for any MK since the establishment of that body. This member is personally responsible for submitting the bill that he has initiated, but one is allowed to use any professional or legal agent the member chooses. Two or more MKs can submit a bill together—any number from two to dozens. In order to ensure an appropriate legislative process for these bills, two procedures must be followed (unlike bills proposed by the government or a committee). First of all, the MK must submit the bill to the Speaker of the Knesset, who then formally "lays it on the Knesset's table" (Knesset Rules of Procedure 134b). Generally, this is a merely procedural stage, because there is no censorship of the content of laws, except for the directive in the Rules of Procedure (134c) that: "The Speaker and the Deputy Speakers shall not approve a bill which is, in their opinion, racist in its essence, or rejects the existence of the State of Israel as the State of the Jewish People." Indeed, Knesset Speakers have invalidated a number of bills which, intentionally or unintentionally, have been essentially racist or undermine the existence of the State of Israel. The second procedure requires that the private bill undergo a preliminary debate prior to its first reading. This debate clarifies whether the bill has a chance of being passed with a majority of votes, which would grant it admission to the order of legislative debates in the Knesset, similar to a bill initiated by the government or a committee.

After the law passes its preliminary reading, it is passed to the relevant committee to prepare it for the first reading, and after a debate in the Knesset plenum for the first reading, it receives a status parallel to a government- or committee-sponsored bill. Nevertheless, the initial debate is one stage among the stages of legislation (HCJ 89/142, 89/172 La'or Movement et al. v. Speaker of the Knesset et al. (*PD* 44 3[529])

The number of laws arising in a preliminary reading is limited by the quota allocated to each faction. It turns out that the average quota per MK is between six and eight laws per year (the length of a Knesset session). The division of the quota within the faction is done in an autonomous manner by its members. Generally, it is divided equally. Despite this, it is understood that a faction reserves the right to grant precedence to the laws which are important for the entire faction or party, such as calling early elections or other important issues.

Bills sponsored by the government—Government-sponsored bills pass through preparatory storages in the various government ministries, each ministry in its sphere of authority. The ministry is assisted by experts from within and without, the legal advisor of the ministry, and the Ministry of Justice (the rules for preparing and submitting government-sponsored bills are anchored in the Attorney General Guidelines, 10.010 and 60.010). After the initial formulation of the bill, a memorandum of law is transferred to be examined by other government ministries and analyzed by outside experts. After considering the reactions and suggestions for changes, the government gives the bill its final form. It is then transferred to the Knesset Speaker and laid on the Knesset table in a "blue booklet", which contains explanatory sections for the proposed bill (Attorney General Guidelines 60.014). The government-sponsored bill is debated in the Knesset immediately, in the first reading.

Bills sponsored by a Knesset committee—In June 1950, the Knesset gave the Constitution, Law, and Justice Committee the responsibility "to prepare laws for the State" (known as the Harari Decision, named after the initiator of the decision, MK Yizhar Harari, Knesset Protocols 5 1743). Through the years, there had been a number of attempts to initiate legislation by the different committees, and on November 24, 1980, the House Committee accepted the decision, according to which Knesset committees reserve the right to initiate legislation, but only when it comes to Basic Laws and laws that deal with the Knesset itself, elections for the Knesset, or the state comptroller. The bill of the committee must receive a majority of the votes in the committee, and the debate about it is in the plenum, as is every debate of a government-sponsored bill.

Table 1: The Procedure of Laws Initiated by Knesset Members or by the Government

The legislative procedure initiated by MKs (private legislation) has ten stages, while the procedure for government-initiated legislation has six stages. At the first stage, and from the sixth stage and onward, the two procedures are identical.

34

First Stage: Initiation and Formulation of the Bill

Identification of the issue and formulation of the bill by an MK or the government (if by the government, it starts as a memorandum)

Second Stage: Authorizing a Private Bill for Placement on the Knesset Table

By the Knesset Speaker, excluding a racist bill or one which rejects Israel as the State of the Jewish People

Third Stage: Setting the Position of the Government on a Private Bill

In the Ministerial Committee on Legislation, or the government if a minister challenges the committee's decision

Fourth Stage: Preliminary Reading of the Bill in the Plenum

The initiating MK presents the proposal, and the government responds. The Knesset decides by majority.

Fifth Stage: Preparing the Bill in Committee for the First Reading

The law is debated in the relevant committee or according to the decision of the Knesset.

Sixth Stage: Debate and Voting on the Bill in the Plenum in the First Reading

A government-sponsored bill starts straight from this stage. The debate is open to every interested MK who wants to take part in the legislative process.

Seventh Stage: Preparing the Bill in the Committee for a Second and Third Reading

The procedure is similar to the preparation for the first reading; this is the final formulation of the bill's text.

Eighth State: Approval of the Bill by the Plenum in the Second Reading

The bill is presented by the head of the committee, after which all reservations are debated, votes are cast, and the bill is approved or rejected.

Ninth Stage: Approval of the Bill in the Plenum in the Third Reading

Voting on the entire bill as one piece, without any further debate

Tenth Stage: Publication of the Law in the Records and Setting the Date of Its Enforcement

Issuing regulations (if required), application of the law, measures of enforcement

The Nature of Debating a Bill

The decisive stage of the approval of a bill occurs in the plenum, but before this comes the discrete phase of processing the bill in one of the ten Knesset committees, each of which deals with laws in the realm of its authority. These committees are: 1) the House Committee; 2) the Finance Committee; 3) the Economic Affairs Committee; 4) the Foreign Affairs and Defense Committee; 5) the Internal Affairs and Environment Committee; 6) the Constitution, Law, and Justice Committee; 7) the Committee for Immigration, Absorption, and Diaspora Affairs; 8) the Education, Culture, and Sports Committee; 9) the Labor, Welfare and Health Committee; and 10) the State Control Committee.

In addition, the Knesset has the authority to establish other permanent committees; it exercised this authority in establishing the Committee on the Status of Women (1993) and the Science and Technology Committee (1997), which are statutory committees. It also established the Committee on Drug Abuse (1998) and the Committee on the Rights of the Child (2000).

Membership in the Committees

Membership in the committees is determined by each party, based on faction size; factions decide who will represent them on each committee. The number of members in most of the committees is fifteen, and some of them have been expanded to nineteen (the Finance Committee and Foreign Affairs and Defense Committee).

The debate in each committee about the bill, in advance of the first reading, and then in advance of the second and third readings, takes place on five levels: a) legal, b) governmental, c) professional, d) representative of the public's views, and e) political.

On the first level, the legal level, there is a procedure for preparing the bill from the professional point of view, so that the committee takes into account all of the necessary elements for the future law: it must be precise, fair, applicable, and practicable; adjusted to existing laws or pointing to the need to alter them; measured in its sanctions and punishments; etc. In order to clarify the legal viewpoint, every committee in the Knesset has a legal adviser, who is charged with the professional phrasing of the law, in preparation for the voting in the committee and approval in the plenum. Similarly, the legal adviser of the committee comes in contact—in the midst of preparing the bill—with the legal adviser of the relevant ministry to discuss the issue of the precise formulation of the future law. This is analyzed, before it is brought to the first reading, by a Ministry of Justice representative as well.

The second stage is that of representing the position of the government, and it is done by the minister or the director-general of the relevant ministry—who express support for or opposition to the law—and through the senior officials of the ministry. This is supposed to enlighten those coming from a legal or professional point of view, and at this time the budgetary aspect is judged is by the ministry's accountant or an agent of the Finance Ministry. Many times, there is coordination between the legal adviser of the House Committee and the relevant ministry's legal adviser, in order to arrive at a formulation which is more professional and acceptable to both parties.

The third stage enlists outside assistance. There is great importance to the fact that the committee must hear from experts in academia and in the field, as well as independent actors, in addition to the experts of the various government ministries. This is accomplished by inviting experts to the professional debate in the Knesset committees.

The debate over bills—whether sponsored by private members or the government—usually commences with an open and principled discussion, in which the positions of different experts are presented. The responsibility for locating these experts falls on the chair of the committee and the directors of the committee, who are Knesset employees and have a status paralleling civil-service employees of the state. However, in the formal phrasing, the committee is *permitted* to invite experts on the subject that is being debated, not *obligated* to do so. Nevertheless, this is the accepted custom, which holds true in all legislative debates. In fact, the experts on the topic are also allowed to invite themselves to the debate, and the *de rigueur* approach in the Knesset is to invite every expert in the field for the first debate, with the aim of hearing opposing views.

The fourth level is the stage of hearing the views of the public; this is accomplished via participation in the debate by public representatives sent by organizations, non-profits and interest groups. These may be large organizations with a wide interest, such as the Histadrut Trade Union, the Manufacturers' Union, environmental and agricultural advocacy groups, and others, who have a permanent communications representative to coordinate their participation in all types of debates by the Knesset committees, but mainly debates of bills. An individual citizen can request to receive a certificate of admission, based on available seating.

The fifth level is the political level, in which the individual voices of the MKs themselves are heard. These people have a central role in legislation, because they are ultimately the ones who have the right to decide. During the legislative procedure, MKs represent the worldview of their party, the parliamentary bloc which they are a part of (coalition or opposition) and their personal worldview. It is understood that MKs take an active role in the debate at whatever time they find appropriate, even at preliminary stages, by expressing their views or by way of directing questions to experts or to representatives of the public.

The legislative process must deal with a number of issues. Let us illustrate two of them:

Dealing with the Legislative Backlog: The research literature points to a great gap which exists between the number of bills submitted for debate and those which are actually advanced (Nahmias & Klein, 1999). On the other hand, the right to present bills has not been limited, with the very process being an expression of the right to public-political-legal speech. The topic arises from time to time for debate, but the procedure has not yet been changed. At the same time, it is appropriate to stress that the effectiveness of private legislation is not measured by calculating the ratio of bills initiated to laws passed, but rather by comparing the number of bills which are brought to a preliminary reading to those which are brought to legislative completion and passed into law.

Chapter 6: <u>The Initiating MK and the Political Players</u>

As noted, one innovation of the present research is the examination of the act of legislation not only as a judicial or procedural process, but as a process of political negotiation. This chapter examines the hypothesis that private legislation in the Israeli parliament is a process of interaction between an MK as private initiator and the government.

Legislation as a process of political bargaining

Bargaining is an exchange of goods or things, a give and take, between two or more parties. Bargaining is also one of the ways to solve a conflict.

There are many theories and approaches in the field of negotiation, examining its goals and processes (Schelling 1963; Pruitt and Rubin, 1986), strategies (Brams and Alan, 1996; Milgrom, 1990; Stevans, 1963; Galin 1996, 2005), the influence of culture on the conducting of negotiations (Bluhman-Golick, 1996; Galin, 1996, 2005; Brigg, 2003; Hofstate, 1984; Lebaron and Zumeta, 2003; Mead, 1994), and the high importance of psychological and hidden aspects of negotiation (Cahanman, 2005; Galin, 2005; Ross, 1993). Most of the research literature relates to negotiations of peace and war; negotiation between employees and employers; and political bargaining between coalition and opposition or between parties. Doron and Sened (2001) claim that in a democratic regime the most important characteristic of politics is the bargaining process at all its levels: between government and citizens, between government and any other interest groups in society, between parties and their supporters, etc. The basic political negotiation is first of all about the fundamental commitments of the states to their citizens: the commitment to distribute scarce resources and the commitment to human and property rights. These commitments of governments are what differentiate between a civil society and a primitive state of nature.

We have also discussed the influence of the culture on the conduct of negotiations – an aspect that has been of growing interest to researchers and is widely covered in the literature discussing the practice and success of negotiations (Bluhman-Golick 1996; Glean, 1996, 2005; Brigg, 2003; Hofstede, 1984; Lebaron and Zumeta, 2003; Mead, 1994). Another dimension of bargaining that has been discussed at some length is the psychological and hidden aspect of bargaining (Cahanman, 2005; Glean, 2005; Ross, 1993). In discussing these aspects, they also related to theories concerning errors and misleading in decision-making in conditions of uncertainty (Twerski and Cahanman, 1995). From the general theories on negotiation, more specific theories on political bargaining evolved, and it is in the light of these theories that we have outlined behavior patterns in negotiation towards legislation.

A great deal of research has been conducted on the reciprocal relationship between parliament and government, including the comprehensive study of the process of budget-formation by the US House of Representatives as a process of political negotiation (Fenno, 1966, 1973; Wildavsky, 1966, 1975).

The Characteristics of Political Negotiation

Political scientists Professor Gideon Doron and Professor Itai Sened (Doron & Sened, 2001) claim that the most important characteristic of politics in a democratic regime is the process of bargaining, with all of its stages: between governments and citizens, between governments and other interest groups in society, between the parties and their supporters, etc. Political bargaining is focused first and foremost on the basic obligations of the state to its citizens: providing needed items in a time of shortage, maintaining human rights, and protecting property rights.

The obligation of the government is what separates between civil society and primitive, pre-democratic society. Therefore, the political bargaining carried out between the citizens and their government revolves primarily around on its accepting or refusing to fulfill these obligations, and this is the most essential function of politics.

Doron and Sened point out that political bargaining is a subset of social interactions, taking place in a domain which we define as the "negotiating space", in which the aim of the participants is to maximize their achievements within the existing limitations—the lack of specific information, or the presence of partial information about the elements which make up the interaction.

The success of the negotiation depends on the participants' measure of specificity in defining the goal, the power of their yearning to reach this goal, and their selection of the ways to achieve these ends. In the political field, there is no such thing as "perfect market conditions," rather the negotiation which takes place is a type of interaction between flesh-and-blood people, within the actuality of the real world. Consequently, oftentimes people cannot achieve the best result from their point of view, nor their full desire; presumably, they aspire to reach the optimal possibility under the given conditions.

Because of the pressures of the bargaining process, and because of the fact that the people who are involved in it have different views and positions, the participants aspire to conduct an exchange with each other, and in this they are prepared from the beginning to agree to the results. Political bargaining involves the exchange of values-based issues, which may or may not be feasible to implement on a practical level.

Doron and Sened count five factors which influence the process of political bargaining:

> *The players:* The negotiators can be two political players, but the number can be greater. In the wider sense of shaping policy, political bargaining takes places on a daily basis, in various interactions of continuous feedback, among all of the negotiators. The negotiation itself is

carried out through many tools, one of which is parliamentary elections. Through the process of political negotiations, the negotiators form coalitions and sometimes even build alliances.

Different interests: Political bargaining is necessary between political players because there always exists a difference in the interests which motivate them, in their worldviews, values, reasons, or belief systems. The possible results of the negotiations are many and varied. The theoretical assumption is that the smaller the gaps are, the easier it is to bridge them, but sometimes it is difficult to determine whether the gap is great or small. These gaps are easier to identify when the differences of opinion bring the parties, inevitably, to a point of conflict.

The end results of the negotiation will be determined to a great extent by the nature of its conduct. The process has different elements and connections: a proper reading of the developments; creating alliances and counter-alliances; proper timing; building trust; showing commitment, loyalty, patience, and creativity; and the ability to respond to steps taken by the other side. For negotiations to succeed, the participants must demonstrate intelligence and experience in balancing these elements.

Mutual dependencies: So that negotiations take place, there must be a common denominator, even when the gaps are huge. A clear and extreme example of this is the Hegelian concept of master-slave relations. The master takes all the benefits of the slave's work, and the slave, for the sake of survival, forgoes his liberty. Granted, their interests are totally opposed; however, by definition, they are bound necessarily in mutual dependency: the master is obligated to mount some sort of defense of the slave because he is dependent upon him for his livelihood, and because the slave gives up on his freedom, he is dependent on his master for his very existence.

Time: This dimension has a great weight at the time of negotiations. It constitutes a key point, whether from a strategic or tactical position. From a strategic point of view, the timeframe is generally agreed upon before the process of negotiations begins. In terms of the tactical point of view, during the negotiations themselves, the participants employ tactics to delay or accelerate the process. There are political negotiations in which the timeframe is predetermined (the date of elections, the date set in law for authorizing the state budget, etc.), but at other times the time to complete negotiations is open or flexible. Sometimes, at the opening stage, there will be a discussion of the schedule.

Stages of progress in the negotiations: In every negotiation, the ability of the participants to maneuver or to advance is determined by the resources available and the constraints imposed on them. In a negotiation which is intensely political in nature, the players are not free to move without taking into account the political powers of the other players. Within the negotiation, they decide which topics will be on the agenda and which will not. Therefore, it is important to craft an order of priorities. There is, of course, great significance to the fact that progress in political negotiation must be achieved in a logical and rational way, so that it may proceed to a better position from the point of view of the political player—in the short term or in the long term.

Political negotiations can end with agreed-upon solutions or methods of enforcement. It is obvious that they can also fail, and then the conflict continues. A failure of negotiation can lead to an escalation or a crisis (advancing elections, a change of regime, war, etc.). The researchers Brams and Alan (1996) stressed the centrality of the element of compromise in order to reach an agreement and successfully conclude negotiation. When a compromise agreement is reached, neither side receives its heart's desire, but if the two sides accomplish reasonable results, based on concessions and time constraints, they can reach a mutually satisfactory position.

Our study yields an important fact: one of the important reasons for growth in the scope of private legislation in the years 1992-2003 is the specialization in conducting political negotiations by the MKs who initiated legislation. Those among them who succeeded in advancing private legislation reached this level because of strategies, tactics and skills that were developed by conducting political negotiation for legislation. The breakthrough came in 1992, and the MKs who led it became role models for those who came after them in the next decade.

First of all, we will inspect the networks of negotiation that an MK who initiates legislation must build with the different players in the political arena who are involved in the process: the government, the public (by way of interest groups), public servants, groups of experts, and the media. Every group has its goals, strategy and tactics in the procedure of legislation—and each has a role to play.

Chart 3: Networks of Negotiations for MKs Initiating Legislation with Various Actors in the Political Arena

A. With MKs

1) All the MKs can vote for the bill in the Knesset plenum at each reading.
2) Members of the committee discussing the bill approve the bill before it is sent to the Knesset plenum.
3) The chair and the Knesset Speaker must approve putting the bill to a vote.
4) The coalition chair
5) The chairs of the factions
6) The Knesset caucuses

B. With the government

7) The ministerial committee on legislation, headed by the Minister of Justice, is of utmost importance. It decides whether to support or oppose private legislation.
8) The relevant minister's stand on the legislation has great influence on the stance of the ministerial committee.
9) The Finance Minister has great influence regarding bills which need a budget.

. With academia and the .edia

*) Partnership with the relevant .mmunities—with experts from ademia, lawyers, research .nters, etc.
}) The media

The Networks of Negotiations of the Initiating MK

With party elements

) The party helps out with public support d sometimes provides a budget.
) The party whip is responsible for getting : the vote.
) The legal advisor of the party helps with : legal formulation of the bill.

C. With interest groups

10) Non-governmental organizations interested in the subject, such as women's organizations, trade unions, etc.
11) Sectoral organizations such as the Histadrut, the employers, etc.
12) Ad-hoc organizations, which came into being for the sole purpose of supporting a certain bill
13) Professional organizations

With experts and directors in the .nesset

) The legal advisor of the committee.
) The secretary of the Knesset and his or her .ff
) The directors of the Knesset committees
) The Knesset Research and Information Center
) The MK's parliamentary aides

D. With the civil-service bureaucracy

14) The legal advisor of the Ministry
15) The department in the Ministry which is affected by the bill
16) Experts from the Ministry
17) The legislative department of the Ministry of Justice
18) The Finance Ministry's budget department and its representative on the committee discussing the bill

The most prominent feature of Table 3 is its complex web of connections and associations. Legislation requires a system for decision-making, containing internal structures which demand the integration and direction of political bargaining with many parts of the network. It is upon the MK who initiates legislation to weave a network of associations and build working relationships, using persuasion and enlisting support in the midst of many circles. Let us specify below these potential ties:

A. *Working relationships between the law's initiator and other MKs*

MKs are the paramount subject of the initiator's efforts, because they are the ones who ultimately have the power to determine whether to support the law or reject it. Similarly, MKs are colleagues, equal in the system to the initiating MK. Despite this, they are caught in a system of triple allegiances: to their party, to the coalition in which they are members (generally), and to their personal positions. Consequently, the onus of enlisting the support of the majority of the MKs falls upon the initiating MK.

Enlisting this support and assistance is accomplished first among the hard-core allies: the faction members, the political bloc (coalition/ opposition), the caucus, personal ties, etc. This is the tool used to reduce possible objections. In parallel, there must be an effort to enlist the support of committee members throughout all of the stages of debate and through the process of voting. The relationship with the committee chair is very critical, because the chair has the authority to set the agenda of the meetings and the power to set the schedule for advancing or, alternatively, holding a bill in committee (in the MKs' lexicon, perpetual holding is termed "burying the law"). In order to lay the law on the Knesset's table, the authorization of the Knesset Speaker is required. In most cases, this step is merely technical.

Another individual who has a key role in the process and whose support is important is the head of the coalition, who is charged with focusing and directing the voting of the coalition members. At the formal level, an MK can challenge the decision of the Ministerial Committee for Legislation through the coalition leadership, while on the informal level there is a large amount of leeway in finding an arrangement with a coalition chair to determine the voting pattern (i.e., "turning a blind eye", eschewing enlisting coalition members to vote down the law—as the chair must mediate between the minister relevant to the law in question, granting permits to offset, etc.).

The faction chair of the initiating MK has a supporting role in conducting informal negotiations with the chairs of other factions, with the minister, with the coalition chair, etc. Similarly, a direct link with the faction chairs, or lack thereof, advances or retards one's ability to recruit MKs to vote.

The Knesset caucuses and lobbies are an additional factor in the process; they come together on a voluntary basis, according to the issues, in a cross-section which cuts across party lines. Their support is expressed in recruitment for voting, helping enlist parliamentary support, and convincing the government.

B. The political negotiation of the initiating MK with the government

The Ministerial Committee for Legislation: This committee has supreme importance, because it decides whether to support the private bill or oppose it. Within the committee, there is a special weight to the position of the Minister of Justice, who is the chair of the committee and the one appointed over legislation in the Knesset. Generally, the political negotiation of the MK starts at this stage, and it is extremely central to the success of private legislation; however, the MKs do not take part in the meeting. Instead, in advance they secure the support of the relevant minister and of the Minister of Justice, a critical stage with significant impact on the odds of passing the law; if the Ministerial Committee for Legislation approves the law, its passage is almost guaranteed, because the coalition supports it (in addition, a bill like this is outside the quota of laws for the MK, allowing the individual MK to advance more laws). In this preliminary stage, there is a great opportunity for compromises and crafting agreements between the MK and the Ministerial Committee for Legislation. Often, the Ministerial Committee for Legislation makes its support of the bill dependent on reducing the bill's scope or changing some of its clauses. The MK is able to agree to these changes or refuse.

The minister of the relevant ministry: The position of this minister has decisive influence over the Ministerial Committee for Legislation, and therefore the negotiation with this minister is essential. Similarly, during the proceedings in the committee, the minister—directly or by way of representatives—decides on the breadth of the compromises and the amount of leeway between the desires of the initiating MK and the committee, on the one hand, and the position of the government, on the other. The minister may also present the guidelines of the professional legal staff of the ministry.

The Minister of Finance: The budgetary perspective is not the sole factor determining a bill's chances, but it has major weight in terms of the considerations of the Ministerial Committee for Legislation. Therefore, political bargaining with the Minister of Finance and forging agreements with him are extremely important for advancing the law.

C. Reciprocal relationships with interest groups

Enlisting the support of relevant extra-parliamentary organizations: These groups—such as women's organizations, workers' organizations, economic or environmental advocacy groups, etc.—play a key role in formal debates in the committee and in the lobbies. Their unique role and contribution is in bringing votes from the plenum.

The support of special interest organizations: These groups—such as the Histadrut Trade Union, the employers and the kibbutz movement—play a role similar to that of extra-parliamentary groups, and generally their advantage is the ability to assist with manpower and the experts who are at their disposal.

Establishing ad-hoc organizations to support a given law: Bodies such as "A Constitution for Israel", parents' organizations, public housing advocates, groups of victims of predatory mortgages, etc., are ad-hoc organizations. They can be focused on a specific issue and not institutionalized, but often they flourish and coalesce into full-fledged advocacy organizations.

Organizations of professional lobbies to assist in the passage of a law: These groups—such as the Israel Bar Associations, the Manufacturers' Union, etc.—have the advantage of expertise.

D. Working relationships with civil servants

The government and the relevant ministry, represented by civilian employees of the ministry, track the law as it progresses in committee. The professional and personal connection with them is of great importance. The prominent actors are:

> *The legal counsel of the ministry,* who acts together with the legal adviser of the committee to formulate the decisions of the MKs on the legal level. Even though the legal adviser of the committee has the supreme authority when it comes to legislation in the Knesset, there is also a weight to the legal position of the ministry. Therefore, the crystallization of agreements and understandings with the legal adviser of the ministry does a great deal to advance the product of the legislation, specifically when it comes to the concrete and applicable details, the influence of which is immense in the character and the implementation of the law.

> *The bureaucrats in the department of the ministry to which the law is relevant* are the ones who represent the ministry in debates about legislation. Their aim is to represent the interests of the executing authority, to protect it and to help the law conform to reality. In addition to cooperating with the legal adviser and the directorate of the ministry, there is also significant weight given to the views of the experts within the ministry (alongside the independent experts that the initiating MK summons). See #27.

> *The legislative department of the Ministry of Justice* directs all of the areas of legislation in all of the committees. By its nature, the legislative department holds great sway in the entire legislative process, in particular in light of the fact that it knows the entire legal code of the state. Therefore, the formulation of understanding and agreements with it is no less integral than the agreements reached with the legal adviser of the committee and of the ministry relevant to the matter.

> *The Ministry of Finance* has great power by way of the budget department and the representative of the Treasury on the committee discussing the bill, analyzing every piece of

legislation from the budgetary standpoint. Naturally (and according to Knesset tradition), the Finance Ministry is considered "the protector of the public purse," and therefore negotiations with it are designed mainly to moderate the opposition and to locate compromises and agreements.

E. *Working Relationships with experts and directors in the Knesset*

The legal advisor of the committee (if necessary, the legal adviser of the Knesset can also provide assistance and/or back-up) is charged with the formulation of the law towards the first reading, as well as afterwards for the second and third reading. Since this is the upper professional-legal echelon, which is charged with the formulation of the law, reciprocal relationships with it are very close.

The secretary of the Knesset and his staff are charged by the Knesset Speaker with setting the agenda of the Knesset plenum. In practice, the steering of the agenda, including the order of legislation, is done by them, according to the guidelines of the Speaker, in cases in which a decision is required. The location of the private legislation in the debate schedule has a decisive influence on the odds of advancing the bill, and therefore, the working relationships with the Knesset secretary and his or her staff are important.

The directors of the Knesset committees have a key role in prioritizing the issues before the committee. The chair of a given committee, who is an MK, has a role which by definition constantly changes. However, the directors of the committee are the representatives of the civil service, and they are professional and stable. Therefore, they often acquire great authority and influence over the years, which allows them to coordinate and steer the agenda and the priorities of the committee's work—even though the ultimate decision lies with the committee chair.

The Center for Research and Information of the Knesset is charged with locating information according to the requests of MKs, including comparative international data. The aim of the establishment and continuing function of the center is to allow independence in receiving and collecting information on behalf of the Knesset, without government interference. The importance of the Center's information is critical when the Ministry of Finance cites outrageous estimations for the cost of the law.

The MK's parliamentary aides work behind the scenes. The lion's share of their role is to assist in the legislative sphere on the level of legal formulation (in particular, when the aide is a lawyer), recruitment for voting, coordination, media, etc. This assistance is very valuable. Similarly, parliamentary aides of other MKs constitute a significant echelon, guaranteeing the presence of the MKs in voting.

F. Cooperating with party activists

The MK's party can help advance legislation, giving encouragement and public support by way of organizing demonstrations, maintaining a presence in the Knesset, and sometimes funding advertisements in newspapers, conferences, etc.

The whip of the MK's party and the other party whips are charged with 'conscripting' MKs for voting. A preexisting relationship with the party whip and with the whips of factions of other parties turns out to be effective and useful, in parallel with the link to the faction chairs. The legal adviser of the faction may help crystallize the bill's legal formulation for the members of the faction, but not every faction has one.

G. Active ties to academia and the media

The assistance of professionals and experts from academia, law firms, and research institutes has great significance. The connections are made by the personal initiative of the MK, and one must invite these professionals to all debates of the committee. When it comes to complex laws, this professional connection is very valuable, both from a technical point of view and in order to serve as an 'Archimedean point' to convince and to confront the opposition of the government and other MKs. It is also important to enlist the support and back-up of independent forms of media. Sometimes, interest groups can assist by publicizing the issue through "bought media" (announcements, fliers; we include an example in the appendix). The media has a very valuable influence on the decision-makers, particularly in modern times, which are characterized by the proliferation of media tools, especially electronic ones. MKs invest a great deal in recruiting the support of the media for advancing the law throughout the process, not only at the end of the legislation. This is accomplished both in an institutionalized way by the committee (a press release at the end of every meeting and debate about the legislation) and in person, by way of the initiating MK and his or her staff.

Chapter 7: <u>How to Succeed: The MP's Strategies vis-à-vis the Government</u>

In this chapter, we will examine the political negotiation of legislation between MKs and the government.

The private legislation process includes several votes of the Knesset: Each private bill must be passed by four votes: preliminary vote, first vote, second vote, and third vote.

The most important political player in the field of private legislation is, of course, the MK who initiates the proposed laws (Marsh and Read, 1988; Mattson, 1995; Olson, 1994). Trocsanyi (1996) controversially emphasizes "The Right of the Legislative Initiative"; the initiating MP is like an "entrepreneur" of the bill.

Fenno, in his studies on the patterns of actions followed by the members of the US House of Representatives (1966, 1973), found that the variables that affect these patterns are numerous and varied:

- **Perceptions**- the premises of the Congress members in watching the individual and his views on the world (Putnam, 1973).

- **Attitudes**- how the individual judges the world surrounding him (accept or reject)

- **Expectations**- the balancing point between the two prerequisites guiding the members of any parliament: fulfilling their goals on the one hand, and maintaining their tenure on the other hand.

- **Images**- how the political actor is expected to act in given circumstances.

- **Behavior**- the way the actor chooses to act according to his perceptions, attitudes, expectations, and images.

All these characteristics of the MP influence his behavior in the legislation process.

The second actor whose participation in the legislation process is critical is the government. Government support or objection to private legislation is a key to the success or the failure of the private law.

In the Israeli Knesset, the political negotiation is with the ministerial committee for legislative affairs: it decides whether to support or to object to the private legislation. If the legislative affairs committee approves the bill it has good chance to pass because the coalition will support it. Within the ministerial committee, the Minister of Justice has special weight thanks to his role as chairman of the committee and the person in charge of the legislation in the Knesset. Unofficial power is in the hands of the

Finance Minister, because most bills have financial implications, so achieving his support is crucial for the bill's chances of passage.

Another negotiation is carried out with the minister under whose purview the law falls and whose opinion is crucial for the committee. Many times in this initial phase there is room for negotiation and compromise regarding the bill, and the committee approves the bill only after revisions in its extent and clauses.

Findings regarding the negotiation strategies of the initiator of a bill with the government

Chart 4: Findings on the negotiation strategies of the initiator of a bill with the government

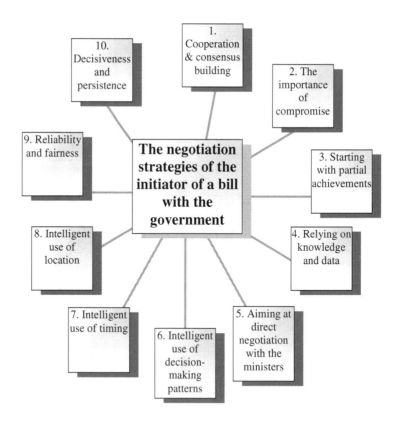

1. Strategy of cooperation and consensus building with the government

All MKs interviewed stressed that their first strategy was to start the negotiation with issues the government agreed upon, in order to reach a common ground and good atmosphere. Only after they had exhausted this path would they move to tactics of struggle and applying pressure methods.

MK Ran Cohen (Meretz) said: *"My first choice always was a consistent attempt to reach an agreement with the government as well as an extreme willingness to compromise on the wording, depth, and scope of my bills. After that, my second tool was to apply pressure. The main element of this was to recruit as many MKs as possible, and to gradually erode the majority the coalition had. The trick is to persuade the weaker links of the coalition to join me. That's how you turn a minority into a majority."*

2. The importance of compromise

In the three case studies, the MKs compromised a lot on their original draft bill by the time the law was confirmed: In the 1994 law for the absorption of discharged soldiers, MK Cohen demanded that the allowance for the discharged soldiers be calculated as 100% of the minimum salary; in the actual law it is only 60% of the minimum salary. In the 1998 law for the prevention of sexual harassment, MK Dayan demanded that the punishment for sexual harassment be 100,000 NIS, and she compromised with the justice minister on half of it: 50,000 NIS. In the 1999 child allowance law, MK Halpert demanded that the allowance for each child continue until the child reaches 21 years of age, and that the additional stipend per child kick in with the fourth child, but he compromised on the age of 18 and the additional payment from the fifth child.

The MKs interviewed estimate that the compromises were necessary. They led to a situation where both sides are satisfied with the legislation passed. This is a classic 'win-win' situation. A strong willingness to compromise is found among all the other MKs interviewed: they mention that in order to promote their bills they do not see things in terms of 'all or nothing,' but in terms of 'more or less.' This is why compromise is an essential element of the legislative decision-making process. Everyone tries to avoid brinkmanship if possible. Moreover, a central aspect of the compromise strategy is not only obtaining the actual results but also agreeing on the need to compromise. The MKs do not see themselves as weak or acquiescent, but see their movement toward compromise with the government as political finesse and as showing a point of view that looks at the needs of the country first. The terms 'responsibility' and 'national' arose regarding all the three case studies from both the MKs that initiated the bill and the chairmen of the committees that presented the bills for second and third reading.

3. Starting with partial achievements

This strategy is a direct continuation to the method of compromise. The MKs emphasized that in the process of legislation one must advance in incremental steps, and therefore it is customary to be satisfied with temporary achievements as a start. Expressions like 'getting a foot in the door' or 'taking baby steps' express this idea. The rationale is that step by step it is possible to build a platform that can permit changes and improvements to the bill on one hand, and to enable the acceptance of it on the other hand. For example MK Ra'anan Cohen (Labor) said: *"it is important that we pass the law for the absorption of discharged soldiers today unanimously and show our support for the discharged soldiers. This is why I am asking all the members of this house who submit their reservations regarding the law to withdraw them at once. If some of these reservations are approved, I fear that we will have to withdraw the bill. Life is built on compromises."* MK Poraz said in the interview that "Always, whenever I stand before an option of 'take it or leave it,' I choose the first option, even though it's not a perfect one. Better a bird in hand than two in a bush."

4. Relying on knowledge and data

Initiating a bill is not only a process of political negotiation; it includes many professional and judicial elements as well as financial and social aspects. The MKs emphasize the great importance of acquiring knowledge about the significance of the specific bill and also understanding its financial effects and cost. In one of the case studies, a big part of the success was the MK's "political-financial struggle": In the 1994 law for the absorption of discharged soldiers, MK Cohen was not scared off by the "frightening data" that the Finance Minister presented to the welfare committee. MK Cohen and his economic advisers prepared opposing economic data and convinced the members of the welfare committee that their data was more professional. It is interesting to note that when I asked the Finance Minister at the time, MK Shohat, about this debate, he answer me diplomatically that "the staff of the Finance Ministry was and is very professional, but it can happen that sometimes their budget evaluation is too high because of the need of public responsibility." That example is significant as it emphasizes the importance of independent knowledge in order not to be dependent on government and committee jurists and experts and enables opportunities to contradict the so-called facts that the Finance Ministry offers.

In the 1998 law for the prevention of sexual harassment, the political strength of MK Dayan and the committee for women's status lies in having a lot of data and expertise about the subject, based on international comparative analysis. The deep knowledge that the academic expertise brought from parallel laws in other countries was a key point in convincing the Israeli MKs to adopt a progressive and modern law for the prevention of sexual harassment. The "chauvinist" MKs such as Zaavi and

Zandberg were "ashamed" to present their resistance to the advanced law and against the professional arguments.

5. Aiming at direct negotiation with the ministers

The formal meeting points between the MKs and the ministers are very few, but the MKs have created a lot of informal negotiation paths. In the case study of the 1994 law for the absorption of discharged soldiers, MK Cohen decide from the beginning that the most influential target was the Prime Minister himself at the time, Yitzhak Rabin.

He could meet him personally, because he was a member of his party, the Labor party. Other personal ties that MK Cohen deemed capable of influencing the Prime Minister were the former generals of the Israeli military, due to Rabin's background as the Chief of General Staff of the Israel Defense Forces. MK Cohen built a civic coalition of former generals and mayors, and their direct meeting and informal ties with Prime Minister Rabin were very important in "weakening" his resistance to the law. MK Cohen believes that this was the most important step in the law's advancement. Once Rabin was convinced, he convinced the Finance Minister, and the whole coalition could support the law.

With regard to the 1998 law for the prevention of sexual harassment, MK Dayan notesd that she built a friendly relationship with the Justice Minister Libayi during the legislation process: initially he did not understood the great importance of the law, but during the formal and the informal meetings, he adopted it warmly and his support influenced other male MKs a great deal.

With regard to the 1999 child allowance law, MK Halpert did not succeed in arranging a personal meeting with the Prime Minister himself of those days, Ehud Barak.

From participating observation it was found that one of the best "secret tools" for meeting a minister face to face is in the plenum. Instead of running after the minister's secretary and begging for a 15 minute formal meeting, an MK may look for the right situation in the plenum, when all the MKs and ministers are waiting to vote and consequently "bored," and grab a short conversation with the minister you need. It is relatively easy to find such situations, and generally the ministers are friendly and the MK can achieve the cooperation he needs better than in a formal meeting. A good MK is like a "good hunter" of the minister's time and willingness.

6. Intelligent use of decision making patterns

A very important strategy is giving maximal attention to and using wisely the known patterns of decision making in the Knesset. Intelligent use of these forms has two levels: the procedural level in the plenum and the procedural level and the informal process in the committees. The procedural level refers to using the tactics derived from the Knesset regulations: delaying the vote until you have the adequate amount of supporters, filibustering, engaging in underhanded opportunism, etc. For example, in the case study of the 1994 law for the absorption of demobilized soldiers, MK Cohen decided to differentiate between the discussion during the first reading of the law and the actual vote. The political rationale of doing so was that on one hand he did not want to postpone the discussion in order to keep the issue "hot" on the public and political arena, but on the other hand he did not yet have the majority to pass the law.

In the case of the 1998 law for the prevention of sexual harassment, MK Dayan succeeded in improving the content of the law dramatically between the preliminary reading and the first reading. She did so under the umbrella of Knesset regulations, which give the committee the chance to change the draft-bill unless other MKs reject it and claim that it is a new issue. The sexual harassment law in Israel is a very radical one, mainly because of the fact that at the first test, when it would have been easier to reject the law, it was not as radical.

These tactics and many others that the initiator uses vis-à-vis the complex decision making patterns of parliamentary procedure give him advantages in promoting his bill.

7. Intelligent use of timing

Intelligent use of timing is also crucial for the success or failure of the proposed law. It seems to be just a "technical" issue, but it is very helpful to identify the right political or procedural timing. In the case studies there were three different kinds of intelligent use of timing:

In the case study of the 1994 law for the absorption of demobilized soldiers, MK Cohen thought that the key element to influencing Prime Minister Rabin was to tap into a groundswell of public sentiment. As noted above, MK Cohen postponed the vote and in the meantime organized civil demonstrations and public outcry that called on the Prime Minister to pass the law. He waited until he found the right time on the public agenda to bring up the bill.

Another kind of intelligent use of timing was employed with regard to the 1998 law for the prevention of sexual harassment. MK Dayan decided to bring up the bill for voting at a symbolic time—right around International Women's Day. Its chances of success increased because the discussion on women's rights on the same day enlarged the MKs' awareness of and commitment to women's issues. Moreover, the committee on women's status made sure to invite to the plenum the leaders of women's organizations and many feminist activists, so the "chauvinist" MKs were careful not to go against that influential forum. The choice of a symbolic day helped the women's status committee to place the opposing MKs in a "political trap".

In the third case study, the 1999 child allowance law, MK Halpert chose the best time from his point of view—a government crisis. Although the government rejected the law, the Shas party (a Sephardic Ultra-Orthodox party), which was part of the government, voted for the law, and it passed thanks to their vote. During a government crisis, the coalitional discipline is loose, enabling the rejection or passage of private laws.

Another kind of intelligent timing is to raise a bill toward the end of a Knesset term, when coalitional discipline tends to be more lax. It was also found that when a bill is raised when an issue is "hot" in the media and close to a prominent public event, its chances of passage increase.

8. Intelligent use of location

The significant element in the subject of the 'location strategy' regarding private legislation is the attempt to influence in what committee the bill will be discussed. The initiator of the bill has the privilege to offer the bill to the committee of his choice right after it passes the preliminary vote. If the government or another MK suggests a different committee, the issue is decided by the Knesset Committee.

The involvement of the MK who initiates the bill in this debate is critical as MK Abraham Poraz (Shinui) said: *"After the bill passes the Knesset plenum, it is necessary to assure that it go to the right committee; otherwise it could be buried for months. I was very active in the Knesset Committee and made sure that my bills got to the suitable committee. If you fail, you can kiss your bill goodbye; it all goes to waste".*

Another element of location is the place where the political negotiation takes place. The formal location is the minister's chambers, but it requires early coordination, and to make an appointment can take days and even weeks. On the other hand, two informal arenas are open to the MKs: the Knesset plenum and the cafeteria. The plenum is a place with many meeting points, such as at the seats during general deliberations, at one of the corners of the hall, or near the couches behind the exit. The combination of many places to meet and a lot of dead time between sessions creates potential for gathering, discussing, and tying up loose ends. The cafeteria is another good informal place to casually meet the other MKs and ministers.

9. Reliability and fairness

This strategy was also mentioned by all of the MKs interviewed. It seems that MKs make a distinction between the political aspect of their work and the act of legislation. In the political aspect they see controversies and struggles as legitimate, and therefore there is tolerance for political maneuvers and opportunism, as long as they accord with regulations. The act of legislation, however, is seen as more ethically charged and professional, and the MKs treat it with more respect; they feel responsibility to justice and the public good. For this reason, the element of fairness is kept despite all the opposing interests.

The basic rules of decency are very important, and every MK tries to keep his good reputation and appear reliable in the eyes of his peers. Consequently, verbal compromises in negotiation are honored by both sides, even if the agreements were never put into writing.

10. Decisiveness and persistence

The MKs interviewed verbalized this point many times in different ways. The act of legislation is a very complex and long process that requires cooperation, stamina, coordination, persuasion, and more. Dedication to the goal of passing a bill can occasionally become extreme; some initiators become fanatic devotees.

The three case studies are very good examples: In the case study of the 1994 law for the absorption of demobilized soldiers, MK Cohen, answering the question what was the most important tool to his success, summarized it in these words: *"The Prime Minister and the Finance Minister understood that they were up against a 'crazy MK.' When they found that I could be a serious political troublemaker, they decided that 'if you can't beat 'em, join 'em.' From that moment on, they tried only to minimize the cost of the law, and I, in order to achieve my vision and goal, cooperated with them. I already mentioned that I compromised a lot."*

In the case of the 1998 law for the prevention of sexual harassment, MK Dayan seemed to be a Joan of Arc of women's rights. When she was afraid that male MKs would succeed in defeating the bill, she asked them personally to give her the chance to continue the process, and she promised them to listen to their comments later. And she succeeded!

Thus, it was found that in order to pass a bill a MK needed to be decisive and stubborn. Nonetheless, the MKs made a distinction between persistence and running a fool's errand. Every MK needs to know how to fight the battles he knows he can win. Perseverance is not the opposite of compromise, but a complementary tool for the legislator.

All ten of these strategies and tactics have great importance, as they determine whether the bills will pass or be rejected.

Conclusion

This study examined private legislation as a process of relations of power and relations of negotiation between the private initiator (the individual MK) and the government as a powerful player. It addressed private legislation that members of the Israeli Knesset initiated during the years 1992-2003. It presents the players in the Israeli legislative arena and displays the findings on the strategies used in order to promote a bill. We examined it through three case studies of private legislation of major laws: The Absorption of Former Soldiers Law (1994), The Prevention of Sexual Harassment Law (1998), and The National Insurance Act (Amendment No. 41 - aid for large families) (2000). Interviews were conducted with MKs and others connected with the legislation.

The main conclusions of the findings are:

1) **The importance of political negotiation in the legislative process**: The findings show that the legislation process is not only a judicial or a procedural process, but a process of political negotiation. As such, it has rules and characteristics, and the sides involved use strategies and tactics in order to improve their chances. Private legislation is a process of interactions and balance of power between the initiator of a bill and the government.

2) **The main strategy:** According to the theoretical literature, there are two main categories of strategies: The first one is the strategy of "mutually profitable adjustment" or the "win-win situation," as opposed to "hot struggle" or "high conflict" (Schelling, 1963; Galin 1996, 2004). The main strategy of the MKs was **compromise**, and the findings regarding the relations between the initiator MKs and the government show that the leading strategies were **cooperation** and **consensus building**, and not debate or confrontational style. The MKs absolutely adopted the policy of "mutually profitable adjustment" and rejected, theoretically and practically, the strategy of "hot struggle."

3) **Variety of strategies and tactics**: Examining the case studies, protocols, and interviews leads to the conclusion that the initiator of a bill uses a **variety** of strategies and tactics, and not just a main one. In each case study, a different strategy was chosen as the main one:

In the first case study, the 1994 law for the absorption of discharged soldiers, the main strategy that was adopted was the use of relationships with ministers, and specially the Prime Minister (strategy no. 5).

In the second case study, the 1998 law for the prevention of sexual harassment, the main strategy that was adopted was to rely on the knowledge and the assistance of the academic professionals (strategy no. 4).

In the National Insurance Law (Amendment No. 41) (aid for large families) 2000, the main strategy that was adopted was to bring up the law during a political crisis, an intelligent use of timing (strategy no. 7).

4) **Priorities between strategies**: In the interviews it was found that the MKs believe that three strategies are the most important tools:

a) **The importance of compromise** (strategy no. 2).

As mentioned, the main strategy of the MKs was **compromise**. Although political life is characterized by strong political debate, the MKs differentiate between the political level and the legislative level. In the legislative arena, relations between the MKs and ministers were characterized by fairness and honesty, as well as decisiveness and persistence. There was a lot of direct negotiation between them. You could find many cases in which political rivals cooperated responsibly and with mutual trust, agreeing to compromise in the legislation for the "public welfare."

b) **Decisiveness and persistence** (strategy no. 10).

This strategy was chosen as second in importance. The MKs emphasized that contrary to many other political fields, in which the most important thing is to be quick and bright (as for example when working with the media), legislation is a long term process, and decisiveness and persistence are key points, as are the ability to work hard and be passionate.

c) **Intelligent use of decision making patterns and timing** (strategy no. 6&7).

The MKs emphasized that these strategies are not just technical ones but have dramatic ability to improve the promotion of bills.

5) **Can it be learned?** The findings show the importance of knowing the skills of political negotiation in order to promote private legislation. This can influence the training program that MKs should have. It seems that acquiring knowledge and skills of negotiation are very helpful. It is worthwhile to examine if and how much of these subjects can be taught in advance, or if they are acquired mostly with experience.

6) **The importance of the cultural and the psychological aspects**: Other findings of the research, which will be discussed in another chapter, are that the legislation negotiation is mostly political, and that is why political interests and maneuvers are so prominent in it. But the **culture** from which the negotiators come has decisive impact on the perceptions of the two (or more) sides. In addition, **hidden psychological aspects** sneak into the 'so called' rational negotiation and have an important affect on the process. Knowing and mapping the variety of influences on and obstacles to negotiation does not neutralize them, but it helps us understand in a better way this complex discipline.

There are of course other aspects which have to be tested in the future. In the Israeli parliament, as in other parliaments, there are members who are included in the governing coalition and members who are included in the opposition. How much this fact changes the dynamics of "political bargaining" with regard to the initiation of new laws, is a very important aspect. Another point is the need to continue research which will examine the problem of the implementation of private laws. We know that legislation is not a guarantee of actually delivering on policy, in Israel as well as in other countries. It is worthwhile to allocate resources to examine these implementations.

The present research contributes to characterizing and discerning the way legislative decisions involving political negotiations between MPs, the government, and various interest groups, are made. This contribution, along lines similar to those of the major contribution of strategic and tactical analysis made by Wildavsky (1966, 1975) and Fenno (1966, 1973) regarding budgetary procedures in the US House of Representatives, is made by the present research with regard to private legislation in Israel. Negotiation theories relating to labor relations between employer and employees, peace and war, and coalition and opposition were used to innovative understanding of the legislative process as a process of political negotiation between the main political actors: the initiating MK and the government.

Chapter 8: <u>Building Power: The MP and Advocacy Coalitions</u>

The Function of the Advocacy Coalition – Theoretical Background

The theory of "networks" deals with the structures within which public policy is formed by cooperation and interaction between the government officials (the organizational approach) and the voluntary interest groups from the private sector (the third sector), the business sector, or the social citizens sector (Coleman and Perl, 1999; Van, 1992). The policy network approach suggests an explanation of the manner in which participants in the network cope with or exercise pressure for changing policies or for abiding by existing policies (Menahem, 1999). Sabatier and Jenkins (1993) developed the **Policy Advocacy Coalition Theories.**

Many researchers have dealt with the importance of interest groups and how they act (Anderson, 1979; Norton and Wood, 1990; Norton, 1999; Rothenberg, 1992; Sabatier and Jenkins, 1993; Smith, 1995; Yishai, 1997). The researchers assumed that the goal of every organization, especially an economic one, is to further the common interest of its members. Therefore, these civilian organizations try to find the best way to achieve the best result. Wildavsky (1966) noted that the recruitment of support networks is an excellent tool for the politicians' strategy. He advises politicians: to constantly broaden their target audience network in as wide an area as possible; to encourage constant feedback from the constituents; to keep in touch and have steady information transfer; to nurture a feeling of belongingness and to invite voters to visit and see the work of the MPs, first hand; to keep their independence and avoid being trapped by their constituents; and to recognize the constituents feelings and moods. The greater the involvement of the interest groups, the friendlier and loyal they will be. It is true that there is the danger of uncovering of the weak points during a visit, but the advantages are immense.

Policy Advocacy Coalition Theories

Policy Advocacy Coalition theories assume that coalitions are built around common beliefs about central subjects. The assumption is that those core beliefs are generally stable and therefore the composition of the coalition is inherently stable. The Policy Advocacy Coalition comprises various players, establishments, public and private bodies, groups, and individuals. Changes in policy are a function of three sets of processes: interaction or competition between coalitions; the influence of a process coming from outside the system; and the influence of systematic parameters, such as legislation and social structure (Christopher 2007; Sabatier and Jenkins Smith, 1993; 1999; Sabatier and Christopher (2005); Kubler, 2001; Van, 1992).

Changes occur in the structure of the network and in its membership. Even when networks are stable, given that the Policy Advocacy Coalition is composed of the same agencies and officials over many years, the possibility of change remains. Policy Advocacy Coalitions respond to the changes in the public opinion and to the results of elections by adjusting themselves while holding on to their central interests (Jenkins Smith, St Clair and Woods, 1991).

There are researchers who assign special influence to epistemic communities, which are based on a network of experts with clearly defined expertise and who are authorities on the relevant policies. The function of the epistemic communities is to develop knowledge, ideas, and conceptions, and pass them on to the realm of the policymakers (Zito, 2001; Haas, 1992.). The importance of the epistemic communities is in their long-range influence over policymaking (which is under pressure of the short-range viewpoint): in creating an overall view (as opposed to special interests); in creating a complex understanding (instead of one-dimensional perception); and in creating an interdisciplinary outlook (not a narrow one). In the modern world, with its ever-growing complexity of subjects and its increasing globalization, its growing number of players and interests, and its high uncertainty – the importance of epistemic communities and ideas in shaping national and international perception is growing.

Yishai presents the various suppositions concerning the relative weight of political interest groups: The group-pluralistic theory assigns primary importance to interest groups in the management of political life. In the assessment of those who espouse the group-pluralistic theory, the best way for an ordinary citizen in a modern democracy to express his needs and wishes is through the mediation of a group. An important empirical study by Robert Dehall, in New Haven (1961), shows that the American policy is shaped by bargaining between groups of interested citizens. Yishai criticizes the pluralistic theory and claims that the image of a political society made up of interest groups is not correct. Her opinion is that "the public" is a group of apathetic and non-influential people, open to brainwashing by the media and by those in power who use their power and ignore the people's will. Another critique views group politics as a bastion of conservatism. That is, those groups that succeed in organizing and influencing policy are the groups of men of power and wealth who are interested in keeping the status quo that serves their interests. Yet another criticism says that in the political process by which an agreement is arrived at between the representatives of powerful groups and higher-up government functionaries, the parliamentary rules are ignored and the spoils are not divided in accordance with objective criteria or fully disclosed. This process damages the status of elected officials and gives more power to the functionaries, whose permanent position gives them unassailable privileges. Another criticism touches on the damage frequently inflicted on the principle of voluntary belonging to an organization, indicating professional organizations of lawyers, doctors, or trade unions, etc.

Yishai notes that the difference between the two approaches is empirical. The question is to what extent do interest groups influence the shaping of the public agenda and decision-taking. Some believe that interest groups, in one form or another, are active in every country, but their political importance is noticeable mainly in the democratic regimes. In the stronger democracies, where interest groups are active, they play a decisive part in setting the agenda. One example is the Scandinavian countries. Nevertheless, there are many cases where public interest is bent toward monopolistic interests.

Findings

Strategies and tactics used by the legislation initiating MK in gaining the support of Advocacy Coalitions

One of the outstanding findings in two of the three case studies and in interviews with MKs was the supportive network that the initiator MK wove to succeed in promoting his private legislation. A large part of the activities of the MKs was strengthened by the help and support of the interest groups. The contribution of NGOs was critical regarding certain laws.

The turning point in the growth of private legislative initiatives was during the 12th Knesset (1988–1992). The change was not only quantitative (an increase of 40%), but also path breaking with respect to the success of the initiating MKs. Towards the end of the 12th Knesset, in 1992, three very significant privately initiated laws were passed: The Basic Law: Human Dignity and Liberty; Basic Law: Freedom of Occupation, and Basic Law: The Government (which provided for direct election of the Prime Minister).

There are many explanations for the success of the above privately initiated laws (Bachor, 1996; Medini, 2004; Rubinstein, 2000). There is no doubt that the central strategy that brought about the law for changing the system of election was the close cooperation between politicians and public supporters. This was accomplished by a strong non-governmental non-profit organization, which ran a massive campaign with the help of generous contributions (Bachor, 1996 – a study regarding private legislation in the 13th, 14th, and 15th Knessets in the years 1992–2003).

The findings (Fig. 1) show the following strategies and tactics, which the MPs used in their relationships with NGOs.

Chart 5: The findings on the strategies used by initiating MPs to gain Advocacy Coalitions support

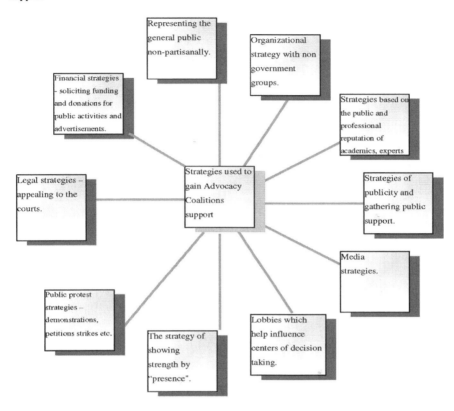

Specifics

1) Strategies of non-partisan representation of the general public

There are NGOs whose apolitical stance can be their strength as well as their weakness. The MPs who initiated legislation used this fact to their advantage to gain support of all MPs, regardless of political differences. This strategy was used frequently and effectively in two of the cases. In the case of the bill concerning the absorption of discharged soldiers into civilian life, a public NPO was established, encompassing a broad public and professional spectrum and representing the whole range of political views. Its membership included retired generals and MPs from the two major parties.

The law prohibiting sexual harassment was backed by women's organizations. Some of them acted as apolitical NGOs, such as the Israeli Women's Lobby, WIZO, Hadassah, No to Violence against

Women, centers aiding victims of sexual attack, and others. Other women's organizations are affiliated with general organizations, such as Na'amat with the Histadrut, or with political parties, such as Emunah to the National Religious Party. But, throughout the debate and throughout most of the debates on legislation aiming at improving women's status, the women's organizations emphasized the general official aspect.

In the case of the law to increase the stipends to children of large families, the initiator, MK Halpert, was not aided by any non-governmental organization.

2) The organizational strategy of non-governmental organizations

The pattern for organizing and gaining non-governmental support was different in each case. The two patterns are:

a) Dependence on existing social organizations

The model of dependence on existing organizations was used with respect to the Prevention of Sexual Harassment Law (1998). The women's organizations are long-standing, having behind them years of experience and expertise. The women's lobby was founded (1987) with the goal of emphasizing influence over decision-makers and lobbying in support of positive legislation. This model copied the style of political activity of the lobbies (especially AIPAC) and the feminist movement in the U.S.A. (Herzog, in Israeli *et al.*, 2001).

This pattern (together with budget cuts) brought about a change in the priorities of the longer established women's organizations. There was less "field work" and more focus on influencing legislators and decision-makers. Therefore, the legal teams and the chairwomen of the organizations devoted themselves to getting the bill passed. Their involvement was first as professional advisors. The legal advisors of the women's organizations contributed a great deal to the legislative process. Later on, towards voting time, they lobbied and accelerated the passage of the law. MK Dayan stated (in an interview in connection with the law against sexual harassment):

> The contribution of the women's organizations was very important. All of them saw this as a central project and invested a great deal in this specific law. I can compare it to the equal rights for women bill, which we were working on at the same time. This bill was less noticed despite its great importance. The motivation of the experts and of the organizations was the feeling that this is a 'lacuna.' We had to give a more qualitative and more palpable expression to raising the status of the woman.

The protocols of the committee for women's status show that the promotion of the bill for preventing sexual harassment was based on established organizations. The department for women's rights in the

PM's office contributed greatly. The Israel Defense Force, through its advisor on women's affairs to the General Staff and her team, extended full cooperation. MK Dayan stated:

> The IDF tended to be even stricter than the restrictions of the law on the assumption that the authority of the higher ranks over the lower is greater than the authority of the employer over the employee both because of the obligatory enlistment and because of the young age of the women soldiers.

> The case of the high ranking officer, Galili, which was being tried at court at that time, was of great influence.

b) The founding of *ad hoc* NPOs headed by well-known public figures as an expression of wide public support

In the case of the bill on absorption of discharged soldiers into civilian life, the initiator of the bill, MK Ra'anan Cohen, thought it would be appropriate to set up a special NPO to help further the bill. Serving as its chairman was General (res.) Moshe Nativ, who had been the head of the IDF's Manpower Division and at the time was the CEO of the Jewish Agency. Thus, he had military credentials, was an administrator, and had ties with the Diaspora. All thirty-one members of the NPO had military and political backgrounds. Davosh, the Chairman of the Association for the Wellbeing of *Israel's Soldiers,* was named vice president. Of course, the NPO was officially established in accordance with Israel's NPO laws and met all the criteria and standards of an NPO. The NPO met every week at the Soldiers' House (*Beit He-hayal*) and helped MK Cohen on all fronts – strategy, operations, fundraising, legal aspects, and lobbying the PM, ministers, and MKs. This help was entirely on a volunteer basis.

3) Based on the professional and public reputation of academics, experts, and public figures

The strategy of enlisting the aid of reputable and knowledgeable experts in the field was built-in and very useful. In two of the three case studies, MPs noted that outside experts had been very helpful in promoting the bill. MK Cohen worked hand in hand with Adv. Shloush, who volunteered to formulate the bill and actively track it in every stage of the legislation. MK Dayan worked with Dr. Orit Kamir of the Hebrew University, who had specialized in cases of sexual harassment in the US, as well as with many other experts from academia and from women's organizations.

MK Dayan stated:

> The law against sexual harassment is an example of a law to which academic knowledge contributed decisively. Originally the law applied only to a very small sector – service givers.

> However, before the first reading, we greatly expanded the law, and based it on examples of legislation all over the world. The Information and Research Center of the Knesset contributed

by locating comparable material. We decided to go for "all or nothing." The advice of the legal experts from academia and women's organizations was immensely important. They went over the legal formulations, which were frequently changed by the legal advisor of the committee, and made enlightening remarks. Their reputations and the international comparisons were invaluable.

4) Strategies for gaining public support

The following strategies were widely used with regard to the bill for absorption of discharged soldiers into civilian life. We can thus summarize that the first goal of the NPO was to generate broad public support, enabling it to influence the decision-makers.

The working hypothesis was that there was a wide consensus on the subject, as it touched the lives of most Israeli citizens – the soldiers themselves, adolescents, parents, middle-aged people, and even grandparents. MK Cohen stated:

> I understood that there was no chance to win the fight from 'inside' – only from outside. I set up a campaign which encompassed all of Israel. In the beginning, we sent 500,000 letters (1991). Two trucks drove up to the Knesset bringing the letters from Tel-Aviv. It was a great organizational project.

When we studied the NPO's operations, we could observe a great variety of activities (which were carried out after consulting publicity experts):

a) **Signing of petitions** – The main instrument chosen to influence decision-makers was massive public petition signing. A widespread organizational network was created and every possible potential site of petition signing was pinpointed. Petition stations were erected at all major public events. Booths where publicity literature was distributed and petitions could be signed were set up at central urban sites and at main intersections.

b) **Publicity – preparing the ground for petition signing** – A diverse publicity system was built, including public conferences, distribution of publicity materials, organization of symposia, etc.

c) **Building a "hard core"** – The NPO acted to attract members (*ad hoc*), to enlist the maximum number of volunteers, and to use the media.

5) Media strategy

In the case studies, two layers of media activity were found. The first was free media exposure, while the second was bought. With regard to the free media exposure, the aim was to circulate the maximum amount of information and also to enlist support for the bill.

The PR personnel in the NPO for the bill about absorption of discharged soldiers into civilian life also dealt with the media, as did MK Cohen's parliamentary aides as part of their routine work. Media coverage of the legislative process was comprehensive. Over 100 news items (including articles and some interviews) were published about the bill (from MK Cohen's private archive, professionally collected by Yifat Inc.). At the same time, a great deal of advertising space, including newspaper and billboard ads, was bought as part of the campaign for this bill (1994). These costs will be discussed in Section 10.

In the other two case studies, contact with the media was ongoing by means that are common in the Knesset such as press releases by committee chairpersons at the end of every session and the constant contact of parliamentary aides with members of the media. The law against sexual harassment got relatively little media coverage. If one looks at the placement of the news items, their length, and the length of time they ran, it can be observed that the law was never a hot media item. On the other hand, every time a concrete case of sexual harassment came up, media coverage soared. The case of the then Minister of Transportation Yitzhak Mordechai came into the public eye two years after the bill became a law and exactly on International Women's Day in March 2000. The trial and the judgment in the Mordechai case had extensive media coverage and led to a change in public consciousness. The Supreme Court ruled that army officers found guilty of sexual harassment are not to be promoted (Kamir, 2002, 2005).

In regard to Amendment 41 of the National Insurance Act (2000), the initiator, MK Halpert, did nothing to promote the bill in the media. The Labor and Social Service Committee put out only standard notices. However, the subject was widely covered in the media because the bill caused a political crisis. Not only did the labor, social services, and financial correspondents of the Knesset report on it, but political correspondents did as well. Because of the extensive media coverage, the bill was passed on November 8, 2000. The coalition broke up over it – one of the most outstanding expressions of the weakness of PM Ehud Barak's government. The government subsequently fell apart and elections for the Head of the Government were held early – only 3 months after the bill was passed – in January 2001.

6) Lobbies – influencing the hubs of decision-making

Lobbying has an important function in the legislative process with regard to each of the political players – on one hand, influencing the position of the government, beginning with the discussion in the Ministerial Legislative Committee and continuing throughout all the debates, and on the other hand, influencing the MPs' voting pattern at each stage, in the committee, and in the Knesset plenum. (The subject of lobbyism in the Knesset is very complex, especially since the 1994 law governing their activities in the Knesset building, and has yes to be studied).

Interest groups act in the Knesset directly and through lobbyists. The influence of the lobbyists has grown since the institutionalization of their work in the Knesset. In this study, lobbying had a strong influence on the successful passing of the bill in two of the three case studies. With respect to the law for the absorption of discharged soldiers into civilian life, the lobbying targeted the Prime Minister and other ministers, whereas regarding the law against sexual harassment, the lobbying was focused on the MKs who opposed the bill.

In the case of the National Insurance Act, Amendment 41 (2000), support was solicited from political parties and not from individuals. Mr. Nativ, in an interview about the bill for the absorption of demobilized soldiers, stated:

> We went to the most influential decision makers, one by one – first to PMs Shamir and Rabin in turn, then to ministers and MKs. PM Rabin was the key figure. At first, he looked at the idea as though it had fallen from the moon. Little by little we succeeded in convincing him. In my opinion, what convinced him was the wide public support we succeeded in generating. After discussions with us every party supported the bill. Rabin understood that it wouldn't look good if the PM and the Minister of the Treasury objected to the bill – as though they were against the soldiers. Evidently it wouldn't have been pleasant to remain alone and he was afraid of the political price. Getting the support of all the MKs and most of the ministers helped.

The women's organizations lobbied for the bill to prevent sexual harassment. They participated in sessions of the Knesset and personally influenced voting patterns of MKs through informal talks with them. These talks took place throughout the legislative period, particularly on the voting day. The women's organizations ensured their presence on November 3, 1998 and spoke to many MKs. In some cases, there were negotiations with those who had reservations. The fact that the chairperson of the committee called a special session before the voting started in the Knesset plenum helped to ensure a large group of "lobbyists."

7) The strategy of showing strength by "presence"

Physical presence in the Knesset is very influential as a show of strength and as a way of creating an atmosphere of informal pressure. There are many ways in which an MK can be helped by the presence of interest groups: formally, by being present at the debate and vote, either in the visitors' or the special gallery; by being present in "the corridors of power," and by being present at the debates of the committees. Both MK Cohen and MK Dayan used the strategy of bringing supporters to the visitors' gallery of the Knesset whenever their bills were being discussed or voted upon. This is a highly influential strategy due to the presence and leverage it generates. MK Cohen emphasized the fact that there were discharged soldiers in the visitor's gallery when he stated (April 4, 1994):

> Look at the young generation sitting in the visitor's gallery. They are the future of our country. Some are discharged soldiers and some will soon be drafted. Look at them...we have to secure their future in Israel.

MK Dayan referred to their presence in her welcoming remarks at the beginning of the session. In these two cases, as in others when supporters were invited to the visitors' gallery while the Knesset was in session, their presence affects all the speakers and their influence is multiplied. For instance, PM Netanyahu also congratulated the women on their presence during the debate (March 10, 1998).

8) The strategy of public protest

The strategy of protest was not used in any of the cases studied. Nevertheless, in interviews with MPs, we found that public protest was one of the most important strategies used to further bills. This strategy includes demonstrations and strikes. The demonstrations are meant to influence decision–makers, and therefore generally take place in front of the Knesset, in front of the PM's office, or in front of the relevant ministry.

The influence of demonstrations is greatly enhanced by media coverage. Efforts are made to interest the media, including various gimmicks, coordinating the time and place with the media, letting the media set the "rules of the game", etc. Another element found in demonstrations is the dialogue created between the demonstrators and the MPs who support them and speak at the demonstration. This strengthens the MPs' and also the demonstrators' fighting spirit.

The best example described in the interviews regarding the use of the demonstrations strategy in the struggle to advance a bill was in the case of the Public Housing Law, proposed by MK Ran Cohen. The demonstrations were systematic and were repeated before every stage of the deliberations. They were held opposite both the Knesset and the Prime Minister's Office. There were also supportive rallies, publicity, and protest.

The leading protest weapon is the strike. The most common form of strike is the labor strike, which lies outside the scope of the present study. For our purposes, the relevant example is the sit-in strike of the disabled in 2000. The strike of the disabled, opposite and inside the Treasury Office, lasted for more than a month. They demanded a change in the treatment of disabled people and a raise in disability pensions. This strike was not held during the deliberations on a specific related bill, rather against the background of a dramatic shift in favor of improving the status and rights of the disabled people. It prepared the way for the law, introduced in 2004 by MK Saul Yahalom, which was based on the Equal Rights for Persons with Disabilities Law (1998), initiated by MK Dedi Zucker and others.

The strategy of public protest through demonstrations and strikes has been used by many organizations, for example, during the debate on legislation on the subject of nature preservation (against Highway 6 and for preservation of the seashore). There was a huge political protest when the bill allowing the withdrawal from Gaza was debated.

9) Legal strategies – appealing to the courts

As noted in Section 1, the relationship between the Knesset and the High Court of Justice is complex, due to the need to balance between the principle of separation of powers and the principle of checks and balances. Consequently, both sides declare that they are in favor of restraint. Nevertheless, if the public or MPs feel that a certain problem has not been solved through legislation, causing injustice or inequality, they may appeal to the Supreme Court sitting as the High Court of Justice.

An example that emerged during the interviews was the Military Service Law initiated by MK Chazan (2000). This law opened IDF combat units to women and was based on the judgment of the Supreme Court in the case of Alice Miller. Another example is the subject of drafting yeshiva students into the IDF. The appellants wanted the High Court of Justice to intervene without legislation, but the Court decided that in such a sensitive political-religious question, the Knesset must have the last word. Thus, the Court "forced" the Knesset to take a stand. A public committee was set up (the Tal Commission), and the Knesset passed the law allowing yeshiva students to defer IDF service (2001).

10) Budget strategy

This strategy pertains to cases when the non-governmental body demands not only legislation, but also a budget. Of the three cases studied, only one came into this category – the Absorption of Former Soldiers Law (1994). The handling of budgets and donations was planned and organized strictly in accordance with the official NPO law. When we asked, the chairman of the NPO directly about managing the budget, Mr. Nativ responded:

> The budget was not inflated. For example, we spent little on meetings as we met decision makers at the offices, not in restaurants. We received small donations from some banks, some merchants, and some industrialists. Members of the NPO also contributed money. When we organized a public affair, for example, with the PM, the hotel hosted us gratuitously. Advertisements were donated by the newspapers. Nuri Inc. donated the billboards. Everything was legal. The NPO was recognized and had an accountant, who was a volunteer. Everything was open and financial reports are with the Comptroller of the NPOs.

Conclusion

The present study deals with private legislation that members of the Israeli Knesset initiated during the years 1992-2003. It presents the players in the Israeli legislative arena and shows findings on the strategies used in promoting bills.

The study deals with the relationships between the MK initiating legislation and **Advocacy Coalitions** during political negotiations. The innovation of this paper is that it looks at legislation not from the legal, procedural, or financial aspect, but as a process of political negotiation. It looks at private legislation as a process involving mutual power relationships between the initiating private MK and the Advocacy Coalition – relationships that fulfill an important function (In the previous chapter, I discuss the negotiations between the initiating MP and the Government, and in the next one I will examine the relationship between the MP initiating the legislation and his colleagues).

This viewpoint brings a new perspective to examinations of the legislative process. The strategic tools used by Wildavsky (1964, 1975) and Fenno (1966, 1973) to investigate the budgeting process in the U.S. Congress were used in this study to examine the process of private legislation. The legislative process was examined (with the help of qualitative research systems) as an arena in which political players of different functions and interests meet. Their mutual relationships, negotiations, and cooperation result in the desired political result.

In this study, we found the political contribution of private legislation. The theories and methods of negotiation strategy, which were used in the field of diplomatic negotiation, in the study of labor relations, and in the area of political coalition negotiations were tested in the relationship between the privet legislator and the Advocacy Coalitions. The findings, which were given a new dimension in this chapter, contribute to the analysis and understanding of legislative processes as political negotiation processes. At the same time, the findings offer a new perspective on Advocacy Coalitions, not just on the MKs.

In this chapter, the approaches and a summary of the theories relating to political negotiation and to Advocacy Coalition Framework and interest groups, have been presented. We observed and noted the interests of the players in the political arena, who were partners in the political negotiations, and built strategies and tactics of negotiation used in the process of legislation.

Chapter 9: <u>How to Win: The MK's Strategies for Winning Over Colleagues</u>

Legislation as a coalition-building process

MKs have the power to decide which bills will pass all the procedural steps and become laws. The support of a majority of MKs is needed to confirm the bill in each of the four readings: preliminary reading, first reading, second reading, and the third and final reading. Consequently, good working relations with other MKs are the first and foremost predicates for the initiator of legislation. On one hand, this might seem like an easy task since the MKs are the initiator's colleagues. Nevertheless, they have obligations to their party's values and platform, and the majority of MKs belongs to the coalition and is subject to its discipline. It goes without saying that despite any collegial relations, every member of Knesset is obligated first and foremost to himself.

For this reason, a study of the influence of the legislative initiators on the process of coalition building is so important.

Coalition building is the ability to create and hold the support of varied components, each one of which of them has its own interests, and in many cases there is competition and even conflict between the various interests. The resulting coalition can be stable or ad hoc. It can be built on the basis of values or interests; it can be homogeneous or heterogeneous, strong or weak, etc. (Tarrow, 2005; Strom, 1990; Wilke, 1985; Lutz and James, 1976; Boissevain, 1974; Neckermann, 1991).

In the legislation process, personal relationships are of tremendous importance, both between the legislative initiator and the other MKs and between the MKs themselves. Lutz and James (1976), in their book *Friends of Friends: Networks, Manipulators and Coalitions*, focus on the importance of the close relationship. In many cases, the MKs are not only colleagues, but friends. What determines the decision as to how to vote (with your party or with your MK friend) is the depth of the relationship. Although it is in the political arena, in which values and interests play a large part, it was found that personal relationships also have a very important place.

Another important point of view on legislation as a coalition building process is that of priorities. The goal of the initiator of the legislation is to have a majority voting for his bill. He has to put his energy into getting the support of those who have more potential to be his supporters and not to "waste" his time on MKs whose chances of becoming a supporter are very low.

Another issue whose importance is critical to coalition building is the connection between lobbying for your bill and the general tactics of the legislation process: intelligent use of timing and accidental chances, influencing the rhythm of the discussions in the committee, and assuring participation or absence from the Knesset plenum.

The influence of culture on the conduct of negotiations is an aspect that has been of growing interest to researchers and is widely covered in the literature discussing the practice and success of negotiations (Bluhman-Golick, 1996; Galin, 1996, 2005; Brigg, 2003; Hofstate, 1984; Lebaron and Zumeta; 2003, Mead, 1994).

Hofstede (1984) defines culture as *"The collective programming of the mind which distinguishes the members of one human group from another... Culture, in this sense, includes systems of values, and values are among the building blocks of culture"* (p. 21).

According to Mead (1994), this definition means that culture is unique to one group and not others, that culture influences the behavior of group members in diverse and unpredictable ways, and that culture is learned and reproduced from generation to generation. Many mediation missions in international conflicts failed because of different cultural perceptions. Western perceptions of conflicts oppose violence of any kind and see it as a counterproductive tool in conflict resolution, whereas this approach has not been accepted or taken root in non-Western regions of conflict. In order to be successful in negotiation, one must be familiar with and understand cultural and ethical aspects when discussing force and violence with two rival sides (Brigg, 2003).

Hofstete (1991) refers to four dimensions in analyzing inter-cultural differences that help us understand diverse behaviors that can be perceived in negotiation:

- **Power gaps and dependence relations**- this dimension addresses the level of equality between the sides. Societies with large gaps are characterized by inequality and the creation of great dependence on high authority. In societies with small gaps the structure is more equal, status is based on skills and achievements, and there is no meaning to age or gender.

- **Individualism and collectivism**- individualism is characterized by the individual standing in the center of society. Collectivism is expressed by preserving collective interests, high loyalty to the group, and self-sacrifice of personal goals to the benefit of the group.

- **Division of roles between men and women**- examining the differences between the genders according to two categories: general norms (refers to family, school, and work) and values and political perceptions. In collective societies there is a clear division between the roles of men and women. Usually women are confined to their domestic roles while men are involved in matters outside the house. In individualistic societies this division of roles is more equal.

- **Attitude towards situations of uncertainty**- collective societies tend more toward impatience in situations of uncertainty and ambiguity. In these societies, the fear of conducting negotiations is caused by the elements of uncertainty: unexpected events, unintentional compromise, submission to pressure, etc. On the other hand, individualistic societies take some measures in order to deal with the element of vagueness in negotiation: information gathering, improvement of prediction ability, relationship control, meticulous preparations, informal relations, use of mediators, etc.

The new literature emphasizes more and more the psychological and hidden aspects of the political actors (Cahanman, 2005; Galin, 2005; Ross, 1993).

Ross (1993) claims that psychological obstacles in conflict resolution do not derive from interest considerations, but more from the way people think or feel, i.e., processes that are not related at all to the negotiation. He mentions four psychological obstacles:

- **The search for justice and fairness**- people tend to waive future profits if they feel that the profit is not fair or proportional.

- **Loss aversion**- people prefer the sure thing over taking risks.

- **Comprehension of information and evidence** that are biased toward our values and interests- as a result, the two sides in every conflict see a different picture, some thing which causes misattribution and leads to a descending spiral of trust.

- **Reactive devaluation**- the proposal of compromise or concession causes a reduction of their appeal to the receiver.

Understanding these psychological obstacles does not totally neutralize their effects, but research shows that it can help both sides. Likewise, momentum for overcoming difficulties can be generated at junctures that make it necessary to reach success, for example, elections or the need to sign an agreement. In international conflicts, the chance for success in negotiation increases when the status quo is impossible and an agreement is a necessity (Ross, 1993).

In this chapter, we will present findings as to which strategies MKs use to build a successful coalition to pass their private bills:

The findings

Chart 6: Findings on negotiation strategies used by of the initiator of a bill to enlist the support of his fellow MKs

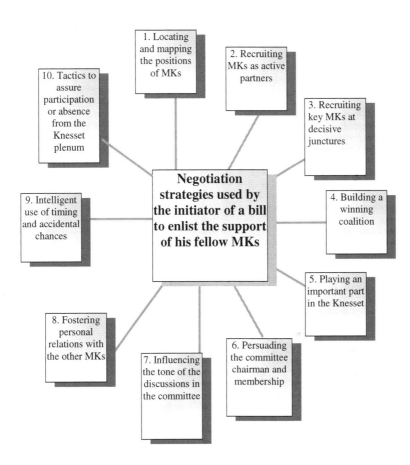

1. Locating and mapping the positions of the MKs

The first thing needed is segmentation of the expected positions of the members of the Knesset. The segmentation is performed on the basis of belonging to a party coalition or opposition, to lobbies, and of course, according to basic acquaintance with the opinions of the MKs. In the beginning, the initiator from the opposition does a rough mapping into four groups:

MKs who are typical supporters: the members of their party, members of his lobby, and his personal friends from all parties. The initiator has to make sure that this "hard core" is really on his side and will help him in promoting the bill. It goes without saying that he has to assure that they participate in the voting. There is a need to maintain relations with this group in order not to lose them during the long legislation process.

MKs who are typical opposers: these are the members of the other bloc in terms of ideology and members of the coalition who must obey coalitional discipline (such as ministers). The initiator treats these people as 'lost causes,' and therefore does not waste time and effort on them. As an example, in the case study of the 1999 child allowance law, MK Halpert could not succeed in arranging the support of extreme non-religious MKs, so, as he mentioned in the interview, he did not even try to talk to them.

Undecided MKs: this is the most important group. They need the most convincing, requiring time and effort to overcome their resistance.

MKs who are handcuffed by party discipline but are willing to help- the first task regarding this group is to assure their absence when voting takes place. Beyond that, some of them might be persuaded to support the bill and to break coalitional discipline on a one-time basis. For example: In the case of the 1994 law for the absorption of demobilized soldiers, MK Cohen, from the Labor party, who was in the coalition, made a "coalition" with MKs from the opposition Likud party, who supported his law strongly.

2. Enlisting MKs as active partners

Enlistment of MKs starts with signing up fellow members on the proposal for a law. This helps the initiator to 'take the pulse' regarding his views: who is with him and who is against him. The ones who sign feel involved and keep supporting and convincing others along the way. The core supporters are the ambassadors of this specific idea in the Knesset from now on. For example, regarding the 1998 law for the prevention of sexual harassment, MK Dayan signed all the female MKs on the proposal of the law. It did not matter whether they belonged to the coalition or to the opposition; this greatly strengthened the bill's chances. Formally, it was a "private bill" but practically it was seen as a bill proposed by the Committee on Women's Status (there are exceptions to this rule, and sometimes signing MKs up does not mean a thing).

In regard to the law for the absorption of demobilized soldiers, 1994, it was important to MK Cohen to lead the law that he initiated by himself, and it did not hurt his ability to build a strong support coalition.

3. Recruiting key MKs at decisive junctures

The findings indicate that the MKs invest a lot of effort in persuading each and every member, but they give special attention to MKs who are also key figures, such as committee and faction chairpersons. In general, the special status of some MKs and their role in the legislation process make them powerful figures. Once these key figures have been convinced to support a bill, it is easier to enlist further support. The chairman of the coalition, for instance, is the mediator between the government and the Knesset. He needs to support government policy in the Knesset, but is not automatically obligated to object to any bill from the opposition. He can choose when to demand coalitional discipline and when to grant free voting. The chairmen of the factions in the Knesset have an important role in eroding the majority of the coalition. When a faction has a dispute with the Prime Minister, there is fertile ground for a 'divide and conquer' approach to achieve the support of some coalition members. Another kind of key figures are those who do not hold a formal position but have great influence because of their informal influence.

In the case of the 1998 law for the prevention of sexual harassment, the women MKs found that in order to break the resistance of the male MKs, there was a need to break up the "male network." When its informal leader, MK Robby, decided not to vote against the law, he influenced five other male MKs, and the law passed on the first reading.

4. Building a winning coalition

The goal of the initiator is obvious: to build a winning coalition in order for his bill to pass. That is why he attempts to create alliances that cross coalition and opposition, divide parties, and ignore differences on other issues. MK Ran Cohen (Meretz) says: *"The object is to recruit as many MKs as possible and to erode the coalitional majority. I used to catch the weakest links in the coalition and got them to support me or at least convince them not to object."* MK Halpert, in the case of the 1999 child allowance law, could not arrange a majority for his law without breaking the coalition majority. He did it with the help of the Orthodox parties, which preferred to vote according to their beliefs and broke coalition discipline.

5. Playing an important part in the Knesset

The interviews with the MKs show that the preferred strategy to promote private legislation is to become a chairman of a committee in the Knesset. The role of chairman of a committee is a senior position in the Israeli parliament from many aspects. The most attractive committees are the Finance Committee and the Committee for Security and Foreign Affairs. From the point of view of promoting private bills, this position gives great advantages to its holder.

In regard to the law for the prevention of sexual harassment, the fact that MK Dayan was the head of the Committee of Women's Status played a big role in successfully passing such a progressive law in Israel. She scheduled the law very intensively in the committee's meetings and acted very cleverly by inviting many female academic experts to the meetings. Another possibility is to get appointed by the chairman of a committee as a head of sub-committee in charge of promoting a specific bill, or to receive authority to establish a team in charge of preparing the bill for discussion in the Knesset plenum.

6. Persuading the committee chairman and membership

The roles of the committees of the Knesset, their authorities, and jurisdiction were determined in the Knesset Law (clause 21) and in the Regulations of the Knesset (clause 14A). According to these, the chairmen of committees have key roles in the legislation process. They decide the topics for the discussions, the agendas and timetables, who will be invited to the discussions, formulate the resolutions of the committee, pass them to the media, and more. All this authority gives the chairmen great power, and it goes without saying that persuading them to support a bill is a big step forward. The initiator can use the support of the chairman of the relevant committee to influence other members.

This strategy was found very useful in two of the case studies: In the case of the law for the absorption of demobilized soldiers, MK Cohen, from the Labor party, worked very closely with MK Amir Peretz, then the head of the Work and Welfare Committee, and in the case of the child allowance law, MK Halpert from the United Torah Judaism party, worked very closely with MK David Tal, then head of the Work and Welfare Committee. In both cases the head of the Work and Welfare Committee was from the same party as the initiator MK. Their values were close, they had good personal relationships, and the head of the Work and Welfare Committee gained political advantages by pushing the law. The helpful steps taken by the committee chairman are very clear in the committee protocols as well as in the plenum debate with the government.

7. Influencing the tone of the discussions in the committee

The members of the committees are dependent on the committee chairmen, who control the agendas and priorities of the discussions. Special relations with them assure that a bill will get special care. A chairman who wants to promote a bill will put it 'on the top of the pile' and allocate a great deal of time to its discussions. Of course if a chairman wants to bury a bill or slow down its advancement between readings, he can do so quite easily. As we mentioned above (5,6), in these three case studies it worked perfectly.

8. Fostering personal relationships with the other MKs

All the interviewees emphasized that personal relationships has a strong influence on the enlistment of supporters for a bill, and that is only natural because we are dealing with people. Nonetheless, most of them mentioned that the bargaining relations behind the scenes were largely practical. Even the personal relations were of the friendly nature and did not rely on business interests. Ethics and ideology generally came before personal relations, as MK Tamar Gozansky (Chadash) said: *"When friends ask for my support I try to help and maintain cooperation as long it doesn't clash with my principles."* The three case studies strongly corroborated what Lutz and James wrote in their book (1976) *Friends of Friends.* All the three initiators of the bills, MK Cohen, MK Dayan, and MK Halpert, focused on the importance of the close relationships throughout the whole procedure: To pass a private bill, one has to go through seven "voting stations" (four in the plenum and three in the committee). One must be able to maintain and build on the personal relations with the other MKs at many points: when there are problems in the legislation process; when discussing the compromises that are necessary; when the bill is updated, etc. The goal is to increase the number of the MKs supporters, and it is a long process of convincing as well as of creating a network of personal relations.

9. Intelligent use of timing and accidental chances

Intelligent use of timing is very important in the formal legislation process. There are ground rules and strict protocols that are determined by the secretariat of the Knesset in coordination with the coalition and the government. Even so, it is wise to take advantage of accidental chances as they occur from time to time. The placement of a bill on the agenda can influence its chances of passing. Bills at the end of the agenda are more likely to pass because of the fatigue and the poor attendance of the MKs. Other tactics are shortening the time of speeches when a majority is assured and postponing the vote to a different time when the initiator does not have a majority at the time. Delaying the vote gives more time to recruit supporters or to reach understandings with the government, which would allow it to support the bill.

In the case of the prevention of sexual harassment law, MK Dayan decided to put the bill up for voting at a symbolic time: the bill was brought up in proximity to the International Women's Day. Its chances of success went up, because the discussion on women's rights on the same day increased the MKs awareness of and commitment to women's issues. More over, the Committee on Women's Status took care to invite to the plenum the leaders of women organizations and many feminist activities, so the "chauvinist" MKs were careful not to go against that influential forum. The choosing of a symbolic day helped the Women's Status Committee catch MKs in a "political trap".

In the child allowance law, MK Halpert chose the best time from his point of view—during a government crisis. Although the government rejected the law, the ultra-Orthodox Shas party, which was part of the government, voted in favor of the law, and it passed thanks to their votes. During a government crisis, coalitional discipline tends to be looser, thus enabling the passage of a private bill that otherwise might have been rejected.

10. Tactics to assure participation or absence from the Knesset plenum

It has been found that MKs use a wide range of tactics to assure that they have a majority of votes for their bill. These tactics include: a request to raise an issue in faction meetings, sending reminders to vote, recruiting committee chairmen, recruiting faction chairmen, a personal request from a MK, sending a parliamentary aide to an MK, enlisting the administrative protocol, requesting MKs to be absent from a vote so that they need not break coalition discipline, and creating apathy in the other side and then coming with a large group into the Knesset plenum. In the case of the law for the absorption of demobilized soldiers, MK Cohen found an original intelligent use of influence: He invited two hundred soldiers to be present during the discussion and the vote on the bill. Their "presence" in the guest balcony of the plenum (as future voters) - was a better "reminder" to the MKs then any speech.

All ten of these strategies and tactics have great importance, as they determine whether the bills will pass or be rejected.

Conclusion

This chapter deals with private legislation that MKs initiated during the years 1992-2003. This chapter, too, demonstrates how the legislation process is not only a judicial or a procedural process, but a process of political negotiation. Another important finding is that the role of the legislator is not only as a "team player" but as an independent political initiator of bills. Moreover, the individual MK is the one who is responsible for coalition building in order to advance his values and political interests thought his bills. In this chapter, we examined the negotiation strategies employed by the initiator of a bill to enlist the support of his fellow MKs. We examined this using three case studies of private legislation of major laws: The Absorption of Former Soldiers Law (1994); The Prevention of Sexual Harassment Law (1998); and The National Insurance Act (Amendment No. 41 - aid for large families) (2000). Interviews were conducted with MKs and other persons connected with the legislation.

The main conclusions of these findings are:

1) **The tremendous importance of personal relationships in the legislation process**. It was found that personal relationships between the legislative initiator and the other MKs and among MKs themselves is of great importance. Lutz and James findings in *Friends of Friends: Networks, Manipulators and Coalitions* (1976) were proved concisely in this article: in many cases, the MKs were not only colleagues, but friends. What determines the decision as to how to vote (with your party or with your MK friend) is the depth of the relationship. Although it is in the political arena, in which values and interests play a large part, it was found that personal relationships also have a very important place.

2) **Variety of strategies and tactics**: Examining the case studies, protocols, and interviews leads to the conclusion that the initiator of a bill used a **variety** of strategies and tactics, not just a main one. MKs are enlisted through varied, intense, and complex strategies which are chosen every step of the way. Of course they change from bill to bill and from one initiator to another.

3) **Priority of strategies**: The findings regarding the relations between the initiator and the other MKs show that the most popular strategies were: mapping the positions of the MKs, enlisting some of them as active partners (especially the ones who hold key positions), building a winning coalition, fostering personal relations with other MKs, and using timing and tactics intelligently to assure participation in votes.

In the interviews it was found that the MKs believe that three strategies are the most important tools:

* Recruiting key MKs at crucial decision points (strategy no. 3)

* Playing an important role in the Knesset (strategy no. 5)

* Using timing and accidental chances intelligently (strategy no. 6)

4) **Can it be learned?** The findings demonstrate the importance of political negotiation skills for promoting private legislation. This can influence the training program that MKs should have. It seems that acquiring knowledge and skills of negotiation are very helpful. It is worthwhile to examine if and how much of these subjects can be taught in advance, or if they are acquired mostly with experience.

5) The importance of the cultural and the psychological aspects: Other findings of the research, which will be discussed in another chapter, are that the legislation negotiation is mostly political, and that is why political interests and maneuvers are so prominent in it. But the **culture** from which the negotiators come has decisive impact on the perceptions of the two (or more) sides. In addition, **hidden psychological aspects** sneak into the 'so called' rational negotiation and have an important affect on the process. Knowing and mapping the variety of influences on and obstacles to negotiation does not neutralize them, but it helps us understand in a better way this complex discipline.

The present research contributes to characterizing and discerning the way legislative decisions are made, such as those requiring negotiation on the part of the bill's initiator to enlist the support of his colleagues and the political negotiations between MPs and the government, addressed in an earlier chapter. These contributions, along lines similar to those of the major contribution of strategic and tactical analysis made by Wildavsky (1966, 1975) and Fenno (1966, 1973) regarding budgetary procedures in the US House of Representatives, is made by the present research with regard to private legislation in Israel.

Coalition-building theories, relating to political and diplomatic coalitions and oppositions, were used to create a novel understanding of the legislation process as a process of strategies taken by the initiator of a bill to enlist the support of his fellow MPs.

Chapter 10: <u>Rhetoric and Gender in Legislation</u>

This chapter presents two important views in legislation: on the one hand, the great influence of rhetoric as a tool of persuasion; on the other hand, the gender aspect of legislation.

Let us begin with a case study for the issue of rhetoric, the debates over the Sexual Harassment Prevention Law. We will present the theoretical aspect of these two issues, and afterwards the findings.

Rhetoric as a Strategy of Persuasion

In his *Rhetoric*, written in the 4th century BCE, Aristotle lays out a broad view of the art of rhetoric (Aristotle, 1954). The work is comprised of three volumes. The first describe the internal structure of a speech, i.e., the rules of argument, and later on its formal principles. In this book, Aristotle sets out the basic theory of three types of persuasion: logos, ethos, and pathos (Chapters 1-2). He also points out the distinction between the three types of speeches: before the council, at ceremonies, and before the court (Chapters 3-15).

The second book specifies the elements of the speech which are meant to influence through emotion (Chapters 1-11) and those which are meant to appeal to logic (Chapters 18-26), which Aristotle defines as the enthymeme.

The third book deals with the material of the speech and the tools of its expression, i.e., in language, style and dramatic execution, which is the last element in importance, according to Aristotle.

We will now analyze the three basic elements of rhetoric according to Aristotle: logos, ethos, and pathos.

A) Logos

The logic of persuasion is similar to that of the dialectic. Both of them are arts which deal with methods of argumentation and debating. They are formal, pure, and applicable to subjects from every sphere. The dialectic is the craft of the investigative argument, which is designed to derive most of its conclusions from the assumption, which is laid out in order to subject it to criticism. The speaker must know how to make true decisions, how to ensure that the truth of the assumption will engender the truth of the conclusions, and how to identify circumstances in which the values of truth are absent.

The essential tool of logic is arguments (the enthymeme, in Aristotle's terminology). Aristotle develops the syllogism (the logical way of inferring conclusions from previous assumptions) and the rules of proof and disproof. He enumerates the use of approaches of persuading or disproving logos (28 lines of argument, Chapter 23), such as using pairs of opposites, correlatives, probability, the relations of reciprocity, reasonableness, statements made against the speaker, relying on agreed definitions, relying on multiple meanings of a word, etc..

Aristotle also determines the powers of persuasion in the ways of logos. He says that arguments of refutation are more attractive to the audience than arguments of confirmations, because they are clearer to the audience: the conclusions "that merit acclaim are the ones which have a visible end from their very beginning." "The ones who succeed are those whom the audience can follow closely, understanding the argument at the same time that it is being stated" (Aristotle, 1954, p. 143). Similarly, Aristotle warns that there are inferences which are imaginary, and one must set them apart, so that no one will go astray due to the methods of persuasion (Ch. 24).

B) Ethos

The ethical side of rhetoric is the side which relates to the speaker as an individual and the speaker's method for presenting intents and beliefs to the audience. The traits of the characters which the rhetoric deals with belong to the scheme of ethos as well—for example, if the speaker accepts or has reservations about a character, whether the speaker praises or derides this character.

Thus, the main issue of the dialectic is to reach, in one way or another, some type of truth, whereas the point of rhetoric is persuasion. Nevertheless, this does not create, according to Aristotle, a huge abyss between the two pursuits. If rhetoric does not seek the truth per se, this does not mean that it involves itself with deceit.

A decisive condition for persuasion in rhetoric is bringing the audience to an emotional state which is appropriate for the issue, so that the speech will cause the audience to rise up, to recoil in terror, or to show compassion to people who deserve it. In order to enable the audience to reach this state, the speaker must be aware of various human emotions as well as the character types that make up the audience. Aristotle enumerates the wide array of emotions, of which the speaker must be able to make eclectic use (Book II, Ch. 1-11). These include anger, conciliation, affection, fear, shame, good will, compassion, resentment, envy and jealousy. Our world of emotions and senses is influenced by our human condition and our age—youth, adulthood, or dotage—as well as our status is in terms of our pedigree, wealth, and power (Book II, Ch. 12-17).

In the end, Aristotle points to methods of persuasion that the speaker should use, such as identifying shared motivations; organizing the opening of the speech; using historical events, parables, sayings, and relationships; employing methods of refutation; summing everything up at the conclusion (Book II, Ch. 18-26). Thus, the ethos is supposed to persuade the audience on the emotional side, while using elements which pluck these strings.

C) Pathos

The pathos determines the strength of the persuasion, and it is determined by the style of speech. Aristotle points to the elements of emphasis in the speech, to vitality, clarity, and fluency of language, to the power of images and metaphors, to the contribution of the meter and the rhythm of speech, and to the essential combination of wit and visualization (Book III, Ch. 1-12). In addition, Aristotle formulates guidelines when it comes to the structure of the speech and points to the distinction between decision and persuasion, speaks of the introduction and its role, outlines the ways to refute prejudices, stresses the importance of narrative and its role in the speech, encourages the integration of questions into the speech, and notes the role of the epilogue. Other rhetorical elements which contribute to pathos are emphasizing the personal link between the speaker and the words, referring to the most senior leaders on a personal note, using Cicero's method of repeating concepts in different variations, quoting lines with attribution, using wordplay, employing analogies based on historical events—instructive episodes in the past, expressing a sharp and incisive view, and using a strong, flowing style.

It is necessary that there be an evident connection between the audience, the message, and the speaker. The art of rhetoric is not mere theory. On the contrary, the true test is the practical application (praxis). The speech is judged according to its effect it accomplishes on a given issue and its connection to a certain audience. In terms of the logical infrastructure of the argument, it is based on the relationship between the speaker and the audience, a system which is unique to the rhetorical situation, and it is the only one which allows the speaker to reach the desired aim of the rhetoric, namely persuasion. As Aristotle puts it: "Since rhetoric is designed for some decision... the speaker must be concerned not only with the basis and trustworthiness of the argument, but also with the method within which it will be presented and the position to which the judge will be brought" (Book II, Ch. 1). Therefore, the work of rhetoric is built, applied, and measured in its success, around the following triangle:

Target Audience

The Message   The Speaker

Aristotle differentiates between three types of speeches, based on different associations and different audiences to whom the words are directed (Book I, Ch. 3).

1. *The Council Speech.* The council deals with issues which are tied to the future. It must judge whether a certain notion will be helpful or harmful. The role of these speeches is to arouse to action or to prevent it. In speeches of this type, the speaker's role, beyond the expertise in professional aspects which is applicable to every sphere, is to take into account the basic values of the society, which are an ultimate aim for human action: happiness, the yardstick of the effective and the good—even ranking the good by distinguishing between the good and the better. The council speech must be appropriate for the type of regime. For every regime, whether democratic, oligarchic, aristocratic, or monarchic, one must adopt the different techniques by which one may persuade (Book I, Ch. 8).

2. *The Representative Speech.* This speech is given at ceremonies and events, and it deals with present matters. The role of these speeches is to forge identification with the speaker and to arouse enthusiasm in the audience. The representative speaker must be notable mostly for skills of praise and denigration, using varying forms of congratulations and different skills of giving advice (Book I, Ch. 9).

3. *The Legal Speech.* This speech deals with issues which have occurred in the past; the audience must decide if the person is guilty or not, justified or not. The role of the speaker is to convince the judge of the justness of his position. In the legal speech, the speaker (just like an attorney in our time) must be an expert in the hidden nature of crime and its causes, analyzing the perpetrators of the crime, the criminal counts subsumed in the charges, the level of severity of the offenses—even knowing clearly the rules of laws and contracts (Book I, Ch. 10-15).

There is no rhetorical speech which stands on its own. The test of every speech is the context in which it is stated and the optimal combination between speaker, message, and audience.

The Art of Rhetoric Today: Continuity and Innovation

The art of rhetoric in ancient Greece generally, and the fundamental work of Aristotle specifically, leave a deep imprint to this very day, in every theoretical and practical applications in the world of the intellect and the practice of rhetoric. Despite this, even though one may see in every actual discussion of rhetoric the development of the conceptual world of Aristotle, the ideas of logos, ethos, and pathos are still evolving due to innovation and constant updates, such as:

• In the sphere of logos, we are witnesses to the far-reaching development of the world of logic, which came to be expressed in the important work of Irving Marmer Copi, *Introduction to Logic* (1953). This book establishes an updated network of studying the subject of logic on the scientific-academic level.

- In the sphere of argumentation (presenting arguments and justifying them), there have been many advancements and developments, which came to be expressed in Chaim Perelman and Lucie Olbrechts-Tyteca's *Traité de l'argumentation - la nouvelle rhétorique* or *The New Rhetoric: A Treatise on Argumentation*. This book attests to the most thorough professionalization of rhetoric, presenting a wide variety of frames and arguments, starting points for arguments, and techniques for deploying them (105 sections).

- On the methodological level, there have been revolutionary changes in the tools which allow the gathering of facts and their dissection, with developments in science and statistics, the technological revolution, and the invention of the computer and Internet.

- The world of rhetoric has been aware of important social and cultural developments, such as the social revolution of the 20th century, with everything that is connected to equality between the sexes. Extensive research literature points to the ramifications of this change in the rhetoric of the praxis of life and media (Dow, 2004; Leibes, 1999; Daphna Lemish, 2000).

- Globalization sets the world of rhetoric in front of a much more pluralistic expanse, and as a result of this, it influences human culture more and more.

It is hard to evaluate fully the position of the art of rhetoric today, in the world as a whole and in Israel in particular. Perelman (1982) assumes that this position has grown much stronger in the late 20th century. He notes that after World War II, rhetorical arts were totally absent from Europe, while in the Untied States, there were many schools for speechifying, but the academic community did not support them. However, in the 1970's and 1980's, the picture changed totally, with rhetoric receiving a total academic rehabilitation, and the world of higher education as well as philosophers exposed the importance and the relevance of it in all of the social sciences and humanities, so that it was no longer a "'monstrous perversion' of ancient Greece and Rome" (Perelman, 1982, 162). He therefore likens rhetoric to a kingdom, since it is does not cover the entire broad expanse of informal thinking.

Irving Copi, points to the importance of studying the theory of logic:

> Logic is the study of the methods and principles used to distinguish good (correct) from bad (incorrect) reasoning. This definition must not be taken to imply that only the student of logic can reason well or correctly...
>
> But given the same native intelligence, a person who has studied logic is more likely to reason correctly than is one who has never though about the general principles involved in that activity. There are several reasons for this. First, the proper study of logic will approach it as an art as well as a science, and the student will do exercises in all parts of the theory being learned. Here, as anywhere else, practice will help to make perfect. Second, a traditional part of the study of logic has been the examination and analysis of fallacies, which are common and often quite "natural" mistakes in reasoning. Not only does this part of the subject give increased insight into the principles of reasoning in general, but an acquaintance with these pitfalls helps to keep us from stumbling into them. Finally, the study of logic will give students techniques and methods for testing the correctness of many different kinds of reasoning, including their own; when errors are easily detected, they are less likely to be allowed to stand.

Despite this, it appears that logic and rhetoric still do not have a set place in the intellectual world of children and youth, nor in the domain of higher education, whether in the world as a whole or in Israel.

Similarly, we must take a moment to turn our attention to the problematic issue of using rhetoric for evil, which the Greeks were very concerned with, as is the academic world and the public sphere in our days. The fact that rhetoric can be used for evil, to promote deceit, brainwashing, and the flourishing of totalitarianism—has not ceased to occupy society as a whole and the academic community in particular.[15] The trauma of the rise of Nazism and the racial theory is a difficult historical milestone, and the famous historian Professor Hannah Arendt (1973) points to the troubling contribution of propaganda and brainwashing to the flourishing of totalitarianism, which commits grave crimes against humanity.

The author George Orwell, in his famous book *1984*, points to the danger of role reversal in the area of values as expressed in the rhetoric of a totalitarian regime. He writes that the Party's slogans are: "War is Peace," "Freedom is Slavery," "Ignorance is Strength." Therefore, just as in relation to social phenomena and many technological innovations, the goal of the art of rhetoric is to strike a balance between the potential positive utilization and the danger of using its power for destruction and ruin. Aristotle points to this complexity when he notes that it is self-evident that one can use rhetoric for the sake of deceit, but this is similar to the use of the body's abilities for violence, and just as the use of physical strength for violence would not be correct, so too the use of rhetoric must be directed towards persuasion in the proper direction, not for manipulation. Just as one should use the body's muscles for creation and development, not for bullying and humiliation, and just as one should use mental abilities to create empowering technologies, not for wreaking carnage and destruction, so too one must use rhetoric with a precise adherence to the measures and the limitations of ethics.

Now, we will analyze the content of the Sexual Harassment Prevention Law, an example of a law which deals with the most fundamental domain of gender.

Objective and Substance of the Sexual Harassment Prevention Law, 1998[16]

In the Sexual Harassment Prevention Law, the values-based view of the bill is already spelled out in its first paragraph, as we pointed out in Chapter 4. The explanatory section is even more explicit:

---

[15] Spiegel (1993) notes that there were authors and thinkers who were notable for the fact that they warned about the dangers of brainwashing and totalitarianism already in the 1920's and 1930's: Stanisław Ignacy Witkiewicz (1885-1939, Poland); Aldous Huxley (1894-1963, England); George Orwell (1903-1950, England); Victor Klemperer (1881-1960, Germany).

[16] The law was accepted in the Knesset plenum in the second and third reading on March 10, International Women's Day.

Sexual harassment impinges on human dignity, liberty, privacy, and equal rights. It impinges on the victim's personal dignity and social status. It humiliates and disrespects the victim's humanity, among other reasons, because of the harasser's relationship to the person as a sex object for the harasser's use... Sexual harassment towards women causes their humiliation in terms of their sex or their sexuality and makes it harder for them to integrate into equal societies in the labor world and in the other spheres of life, and thus it impinges on their equality. Relating to them only as sex objects impinges on their social and intellectual status.

As we noted, the concept of sexual harassment is based on the ideas promoted by Catharine MacKinnon in the United States in the 1970's. Its definition—impinging on equality and personal dignity, undermining the woman's self-esteem, committing a criminal offense against women—was a great accomplishment for the concept of equality between the sexes. For the first time, a legal category was created by women in order to safeguard their rights.

Orit Kamir (2005) has already pointed out the significance of the Israeli Hebrew term *kavod*: it does not have one definition, but rather a number of different senses contained within it, so that in English we need to employ four different definitions: honor, glory, dignity and respect.

This pluralism of content of the term is not merely semantic; it attests to the fact that the Israeli Hebrew value of human *kavod* actually has four discrete facets. These meanings are not only not synonymous; sometimes, they are mutually exclusive and contradictory.

• **Honor** refers to the social status, structured according to social order and class hierarchy. A sense of honor causes one to act in an honorable manner. It is not acceptable to dishonor someone who is honorable. On the other hand, denigrating the other's honor increases the honor of the attacker at the victim's expense. The difference between male and female honor in Middle Eastern society is great; honor is a game for warrior males, while female sexuality has the potential for embarrassment and constantly endangers male honor.

• **Glory** is the word used by most Scriptural translations in the English language to describe most of the expressions of *kavod*, which relate to God. The connection to God gives this *kavod* a touch of magnificence, splendor, beauty, grandeur, royalty, awe, and praise. In the interpersonal connection, the glory of a person gives him or her rights which reflect the obligations which fall on others because of the image of God in him or her. In this meaning, warrior males may exude glory, but cases of abortion, masturbation, gay sex, infidelity, and suicide are examples of acts which impinge on this glory.

• **Dignity** is the modern concept which developed in the cultural humanist tradition at the time of the Enlightenment and in particular as a result of World War II, and it is written as part of the first article of the Universal Declaration of Human Rights adopted by the United Nations in 1948, which states that "All human beings are born free and equal in dignity and rights." Its aim is to mark a red line in human actions which cannot be crossed under any circumstances. The dignity of humans sets them apart from other creatures, but it does not necessarily raise or lower them in relation to others, as opposed to honor, in terms of which a person's status and reputation are determined in relation to others.

• **Respect**: The meaning of the English word respect is the aspect of *kavod* which expresses tolerance towards every person, his characteristics and unique needs as he himself defines them. This is a deep form of acceptance, despite the different and unique characteristics of each individual, out of compassion and a minimum of prejudice. The concept is close to dignity, but there is significance to the distinction; the feeling of respect can enrich the concept of dignity.

The Sexual Harassment Prevention Law sought (successfully) to bring about a conceptual and cultural revolution in the ideas of *kavod* and heroism. Unlike the mentality of glory and honor, which arouses competition and aggression, the advocates of which are motivated by fear of shame and humiliation, respect and dignity encourage partnership and mutual concern, and their adherents are motivated by solidarity, universal humanity, concern, and empathy. The State of Israel, born in the Zionism of glory and honor, wanted to adopt a law opposing sexual harassment in which the *kavod* of humans and the *kavod* of the woman would be the *kavod* of respect and dignity.

This was a social-cultural-philosophical revolution. The law was very significant in light of the fact that in Israel, as in many countries, sexual harassment was considered but a minor, trivial, and non-harmful annoyance. It was often seen as an expression of masculinity.

Substance of the Sexual Harassment Prevention Law

A summation of the clauses of the law are:

1.   **The objective of the law** is defined in a broad, inclusive way: "The purpose of this law is to prohibit sexual harassment in order to defend human dignity, freedom, and privacy and in order to promote equality between the sexes."

2.   **Definitions** are the explanations of the terms and organizational frameworks to which the law refers.

3.   **Sexual harassment and persecution** are defined as follows:

(a) (1) extortion by threat, when the act that the person is required to perform is of a sexual nature; (2) indecent acts; (3) repeated propositions of a sexual nature, addressed to a person who has demonstrated to the harasser that he or she is not interested in the said propositions; (4) repeated references addressed to a person and focused on his or her sexuality, when that person has demonstrated to the harasser that he or she is not interested in the said references; (5) an insulting or debasing reference to a person in connection with his or her gender or sexuality, including his or her sexual preference; (6) propositions or references... even if the harassed person has not demonstrated to the harasser that he or she is not interested in the said propositions or references; (a) toward a minor or helpless person, by exploiting a disciplinary, educational or treatment relationship; (b) toward a patient within the framework of psychological or medical treatment, by exploiting the patient's dependence on the person

90

treating him or her; (c) toward an employee within the framework of an employment relationship, and toward a person in service within the framework of such service, by exploitation of authority and discipline in labor relations or in the service.

(b) Persecution is any harm stemming from sexual harassment or from a complaint or an action brought because of sexual harassment.

The list in (a) (6) was later extended to those in National Service; students between grades 12 and 14, even if they are not minors; and lecturer-student relationships.

4.   **Prohibition**—this clause forbids sexual harassment.

5.   **Sexual harassment and persecution as offenses.**

5. (a) Where a person harasses another sexually, as provided in Section 3(a)(3) to (6), he shall be liable to 2 years imprisonment.

(b) Where a person persecutes another, as provided in Section 3(b) he shall be liable to 3 years imprisonment.
(c) Where a person has harassed another sexually as provided in subsection (a) and has persecuted such person as provided in subsection (b) he shall be liable to 4 years imprisonment.

6.   **Sexual harassment and persecution are civil wrongs:** "The Court may award compensation of up to NIS 50,000 for sexual harassment and persecution, without proof of damage."

7.   **Action to be taken by the employer.** The employer must "take effective action in cases of sexual harassment or persecution" and make sure that the employees know the rules for proper conduct

8.   **Failure to publicize a set of rules is an offense.** The employer can be fined for failing to publicize the rules.

9.   **Expansion of applicability** makes a person employed through a contractor a full employee for these issues.

10.   **Powers of the Labor Court**—this is the address for all civil proceedings.

11.-18. These are administrative and legal clauses, naming the Minister of Justice as the one responsible for implementing all of these laws: "The Minister of Justice is charged with the implementation of this Law and he may, with the approval of the Knesset Committee for the Advancement of the Status of Women, make regulations on any matter relating to its implementation" (Clause 13).

Research and Findings: MKs' Use of Rhetorical Tools in the Debate about the Sexual Harassment Prevention Law

In my research, I investigated the use of rhetoric in the Sexual Harassment Prevention Law deliberated in the Knesset in 1997-8. The research was conducted using the content analysis method: I examined the speeches of MKs in accordance with rhetorical methods, and I categorized the arguments they raised based on criteria of persuasiveness. Additionally, I relied upon the frequency with which the statements appeared.

The research was conducted on discussions in the Knesset plenum, not in the committee that deliberated the law—the Committee for the Status of Women. The main findings of the research follows.

The MK's best available time for formal persuasion is the plenum speech. Research has revealed (Maor, 2007) that MKs have been quite clever in making professional and systematic use of their speeches from upon this stage. Further on we will dissect some of them, without taking anything away from the worth and the importance of the other formal or informal areas of persuasion such as Knesset committees, factions, and persuasive "one-on-one" discussions, which are also important and effective. With this, the initiators of the laws built their speeches upon presenting the bill in the Knesset plenum precisely, as did many MKs when they took a part in the debates about the laws in the first reading, and about the reservations in the second and third readings. Dissecting the content of the speeches, we will point out the strategies of persuasion and the diverse reasoning system which the MKs used.

Chart 7: Rhetoric as Employed by Members of Knesset Initiating Legislation

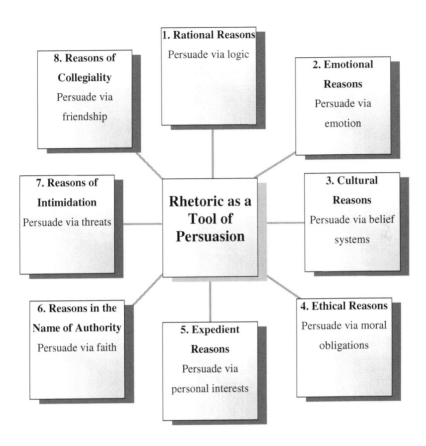

Let us examine the findings of the use of every one of these strategies of persuasion:

1. Rational Reasons

Aristotle and others stress logos as an essential tool in the work of persuasion. Copi (19) determines that the use of a "logical" explanation as opposed to an "illogical" explanation or "logical thinking" as opposed to "illogical thinking" relates to the concept of "logical" as intelligent. Even if the speakers and the listeners are not talking about inspecting the validity of the arguments in the classic sense of logic, they are more thoroughly convinced, scientifically and intuitively, if the arguments are presented in a logical and rational way. The initiators of the laws, who requested the support of their fellow MKs, chose to raise rational reasons, turning to the common denominator of argumentation.

For example, the main aim of the Sexual Harassment Prevention Law is to protect the principle of human dignity and to prevent impingement on human dignity, and it merited the support of MK Benny Elon, who was not part of the political camp of the law's initiators:

> This is a very important law. It is good that it reaches the Knesset table... We are taking a part here in the creation of a new norm of mutual respect; a woman is not a sexual object, and it cannot be that there will be a cultural style that relates to a woman as a sexual object, when she says "Don't speak to me like that." This is logical, this is self-evident, this is respectful, and this is Jewish. I will support this law, because it is a law of human dignity
>
> (Knesset Protocols July 9, 1997)

2. *Emotional Reasons*

Aristotle stresses (Book II) that a consequential condition of persuasion in a speech is bringing the audience to an emotionally advantageous position for the issue, so that the speaker causes the listeners to be riled up by things that the speaker finds outrageous, to tremble at things that the speaker sees as a threat, or to show compassion to people worthy of pity. In order for the audience to reach this state, the speaker must exhibit different human emotions, just as the character types who make up the audience exhibit different emotions.

An analysis of the content of the speeches which MKs made shows that they gave a respectable place to emotional reasons. There is no way of knowing if this was a premeditated or intuitive choice. It appears that there was the integration of both elements. Yael Dayan stressed the emotional side four times in her various speeches, and she argued with those who take the phenomenon of sexual harassment lightly, when she said (Knesset Protocols, July 29, 1997):

> I want to preface this and say that I am proud of the fact that the grins that greeted this law in the previous Knesset have perished from the Earth. Today, I do not stand here in a state of half-embarrassment while from the audience they say to me: "Wait a second, I can't say 'Sweetie'?" "If I pinch, then romance is dead, and it will be forbidden to court?" It will be permissible to court, my male friends and my female friends, the MKs. It is allowed to court, it is allowed to love, it is allowed to have sex, it is allowed to do all of these things when they are done with consent. When one side refuses the first time and the harasser continues to harass under any circumstances, and once again there is a refusal of any sort, whether I or you say no, we mean no.

3. *Cultural Reasons*

As we have seen, the researchers today relate an increasing importance to the issue of the influence of cultural difference on the ability to influence and to conduct negotiations. The cultural reasoning system fulfills a more central role in debates about the Sexual Harassment Prevention Law. This is made manifest both by the initiators of the law and by its opponents. MK Reuven Rivlin expressed the cultural dimension when he said (ibid.):

> I have lived by the songs, "Hey, doll, sweetie, let's get a drink," as something self-evident. We would say this to every woman. The woman is not a doll, but the environment was like this, because this is how we acted, and no one was ever offended at the time when we said that.

MK Benny Elon said (ibid.):

> They won't call me "Sweetie," and they will not suggest to me, "Come sleep with me" out of the blue when they pass me in the hall. But it is accepted when a woman is addressed this way. Why? Because she is a woman... I do not accept this. I think that this law is in the proper place at the proper time, and that is how it should be.

MK Rechavam Ze'evi presented the opposite approach (ibid.):

> Those who set out this law have forgotten the accepted norm between man and woman. The woman loves that they court her. The first time she will say no, but perhaps the third time she will say yes. The woman loves this; this is the experience of life. Read books, watch movies, look at your own biographies.

In the debate of the second reading (Knesset Protocols, March 10, 1998), MK Ze'evi chose to make wide use of cultural reasons, quoting the Bible and other Jewish sources:

> "Return, return, O Shulammite... your belly is like a heap of wheat set about with lilies. Your two breasts are like two fawns, twins of a gazelle. Your neck is as a tower of ivory... How fair and how pleasant are you, O love, for delights! This, your stature, like a palm-tree, and your breasts like clusters of grapes... let your breasts be as clusters of the vine, and the smell of your countenance like apples; And the roof of your mouth like the best wine" (Song of Songs 7:1-10)—these are the words. Now it all goes straight to the prosecution!

In other words, Ze'evi indicts the initiators of the law for leading to a situation in which words of love and courting, as they were expressed in the Bible for example, will be understood as sexual harassment, and it will constitute grounds for criminal prosecution.

Another use of a cultural tool was when MK Ze'evi referred to a film which had been broadcast on Channel 2, in which one of the bosses tells his female employee: "*Hatzitzi ha-hutza*", "look outside." MK Ze'evi explained:

> He meant to ask her to look outside [*hatzitzi*—imperative feminine conjugation for "look"], but she understood it in a totally different way [*ha-tzitzi* being slang for "the tit"]. From that moment, a demonic dance began, a process started down a torturous path; he was forced to stop working, to sell his house in order to hire lawyers; his wife and children left him. A public assault was launched against him, and all of them said: "How dare he say to his secretary '*Ha-tzitzi ha-hutza*'"? But all he said was: "*Hatzitzi ha-chutza*"—"Look outside"!

> Therefore, at this time I summarize and say: there are norms in our society, which is a mixed and open society, and I ask you, the initiators, do you want to create fences, to put a halt to the courting, so that it will be forbidden to compliment, forbidden to invite, forbidden to lust? I

have already said: read literature, see movies, see how people fall in love, see how they court. We cannot pass laws to deal with negligible, marginal cases and to make decrees against the entire community. I ask the initiators: what are you striving for? It may be that you will defend yourselves from a difficult, invalid, evil occurrence here and there, but you will create an atmosphere of segregation between the sexes. Is this what you intend? I am certain that you do not. This is because I know the initiators, and I know that they are all enlightened and progressive. They did not intend this.

He concluded his words by declaring:

I am for the law, but I am for its being balanced and for its not making us ridiculous. In my view, the initiator or initiators have gone too far with their paragraphs and subparagraphs, so much so that this law has become diabolical... As I have said, I am opposed to a law which will cause people to disrespect the law, because there is an exaggeration here, and every exaggeration has in it an intent which crosses a boundary.

In the use of cultural systems of reasoning, we find that there is a repeated use of the base of shared socialization such as the Bible, Jewish tradition, Zionism, and the military experience. Everyone takes from it the cultural values which express his or her worldview.

4. Ethical Reasons

Ethics have a significant weight in the creation of social agreements and the ability to persuade. The use of ethical reasons is aimed at strengthening the power of the legitimization and the feeling of collective responsibility. Beyond this, specifically because of the bitter experience of using rhetoric for evil, the sensitivity to this issue is very high. As we have said, Spiegel (1993) points to the problems and dangers which are involved with using language for evil, particularly the use of it for brainwashing; he notes that authors and thinkers struggled against the negative use of language in the decades before World War II. Despite this, when examining the debates about the Sexual Harassment Prevention Law, we may note that the use of ethical reasons was in the context of the contents of the law. The speakers stressed that the nature of the law is entirely ethical: maintaining the dignity, liberty, and sovereignty of women, not merely the "technical" issue of harassment.

5. Reasons of Expedience

The strategy of expedient reasons appears in Aristotle's lines of reasoning. He notes that in order to persuade, the speaker must

test what arouses to action and what prevents it, what motives make people take action or avoid taking action... if it helps the actor or the actor's friends, or if it causes damage or pain to enemies, or if its damage (to the actor) is less than the anticipated benefit—on the basis of this, one is encouraged to take action; while on the basis of its opposite, one is dissuaded.

(Aristotle, 1954, p. 141)

In the area of expedient reasons, the MKs stressed that the prevention of sexual harassment will not only safeguard women's dignity, but that sovereign, independent, confident, and opinionated women would be able to contribute to society to a much greater extent, whether in the workplace or in family life. The law therefore would not just prevent injustice and discrimination; it would enhance the prosperity of the society and the economy.

6. Reasons that Appeal to Authority

The need for authority is a deep personal and societal need. It has both psychological and sociological sources, but we do not have the space to deal with them. However, human history points to the power of religious authority, the deep desire for belonging, and the decisive influence of national authority, parental authority, scientific and professional authority, etc. A large part of explicating the success of totalitarianism is hidden in the admiration and even apotheosis applied to the leader (Arendt, 1973).

Part of the powerbase of authority has already been presented in the cultural reasoning system: the use of the powerbase of the shared socialization of the Bible and the Jewish tradition. Another source of authority which MKs used as support for the Sexual Harassment Prevention Law is the High Court of Justice. The ruling of the Supreme Court, which was accepted one day before the passing of the bill in the Knesset (March 9, 1998), was the subject of much valuable reference at the time of the debate in the Knesset. Five MKs who spoke mentioned it as an important basis for the law. For example, MK Naomi Chazan declared (Knesset Protocols, March 10, 1998): "Mr. Member of Knesset Ze'evi, Supreme Court Justice Yitzhak Zamir responded to you in a learned verdict, which the Honorable President of the Supreme Court Aharon Barak and the Honorable Justice Tova Strasberg-Cohen joined."

An additional source of authority is "the nation" or "the people". Apparently, this body is anonymous; nonetheless, it expresses the "general will" (which Jean-Jacques Rousseau, in his book *On the Social Contract*, 1967, discusses). Therefore, the assumption is that "the nation" or "the people" are a greatly influential source. Examples of the use made of this source are: "I want help from all of you, so that women will file a complaint, because they do not do so presently," MK Yael Dayan stated (July 29, 1997), in the name of "all women".

Thus, MKs make broad use of references to external sources of authority who reinforce their arguments.

7. Reasons of Intimidation

Fear is one of the tools that Aristotle counts for influencing emotions (Book II, Ch. 5). He defines fear as "pain or distress emanating from the image of some unexpected evil associated with pain or loss" (p. 106). Something frightens us when there are signs that it is likely to occur. The opposite feeling of fear is security, and therefore people tend to settle themselves in situations which will give them security and distance themselves from situations of danger. Despite this, those who support a totalitarian regime believe that the imposition of fear, sanctions, and punishments upon people constitutes an important tool of persuasion.

In debates about laws, we have not found a direct use of instilling fear or terror as a tool of persuasion. Despite this, there are situations in which MKs prefer to integrate in their strategy of cooperation a strategy of struggle and intimidation, but this carries a political character, not a personal one. It turns out that "threatening" reasons are part of the totality, and their integration into the debate is done in a directed and structured way during intermediate readings.

When it comes to the Sexual Harassment Prevention Law, 1998, there were exchanges during the intermediate readings which raised the issue of "intimidation" (ibid.)

> MK RECHAVAM ZE'EVI (from the speaker's podium): I listened to the entire debate, and I will definitely vote against the law.
>
> MK TAMAR GOZANSKY: It is good that we know who will vote against. It is good that we know who is who. Great.
>
> MK ZE'EV BOIM: Don't make threats!
>
> MK GOZANSKY: I'm not making threats. I want to know what people's opinions are.
>
> MK BOIM: Without fear and without bias.
>
> MK GOZANSKY: Yes, definitely. After all, when you harass, you are not afraid.

8. Reasons of Collegiality

Another set of reasons that MKs use is turning to their colleagues with a request to support a bill, ignoring political or personal considerations. For example, MK Yael Dayan (who was concerned that the bill would not pass the first reading because of its many opponents in the debate) said (July 29, 1997—the emphases are mine):

> People who oppose this law—I am prepared, perhaps on a day when we have more time, to try to persuade you. **I ask: do not vote down this law**. Let us pass it in the first reading... I will accept any note, with all due respect and with all due seriousness of the debate, as I will accept reservations. The law is a law which will receive the government's approval, **and I beg of you**...

Summary

The research examined the various strategies of persuasion employed for the Sexual Harassment Prevention Law in Israel, 1998. The findings indicate that MKs, women and men alike, employed a variety of rationales, not a single method. They used both rational and emotional reasons, with a preference indicated for emotional and cultural reasons. It was also found that since this was such a divisive issue, there was no small amount of recourse to sources of authority such as the Bible and the Supreme Court. I believe that this choice on the part of the MKs was adapted to the target of their persuasions—each MK has his own belief system, and thus must be approached with a different strategy of persuasion.

In a different study, in which I compared the rhetorical strategies employed during the deliberations of three laws, it was found that use of different strategies of persuasion changes from law to law, and there are laws in which the stresses were specifically rational, while in others it was emotional, threatening, or otherwise. Despite this, it appears that there were different integrations and combinations, and there was no reliance on one strategy of persuasion.

Legislation and Gender: The Contribution of Female MKs to Israeli Lawmaking

Another important gender aspect is the comparison between the legislative activity of female and male MKs. Newman and Sheth (1987) find that the more that women's political power increases, the more they tend to be involved politically in issues on the public agenda. According to Berkman and O'Connor (1993), Vega and Firestone (1995), Barrett (1997), and Dolan & Ford (1995), in studies which equate the behavior and the activities of female parliamentarians to those of their male counterparts, a difference of behavior is revealed between men and women. In Israel, a study done by ISEF (the International Sephardic Education Foundation) of parliamentary activity in Israel (2002) found that five of eleven leading MKs in social legislation were women. Galin (1996) points to the differences in conducting negotiations between women and men (pp. 274-276). Ben Aryeh (1999) writes: "The results of this study clearly confirm the assumption that the sex of an MK is tied to and influences the measure of activity in general, and the activity on issues of welfare specifically—and that women are more active than men" (p. 99). Equating the legislative initiatives of female MKs vs. male MKs in the years 1992-2003 indicates incomparably greater intensive activity by female MKs in two of three tenures analyzed.

Chart 8: Findings: Initiating Legislation by Gender of MK

Total Private Laws	Total Women in the Knesset		Women Initiating Legislation		Years of Term
	Percentage	Number	Percentage	Numbers of Laws	
250	9%	11	9%	23	1996 -1992
138	8%	9	15%	21	1999 -1996
235	12%	15	24%	57	2003 -1999
623	10%	34	16%	101	Total

Thus, the findings are that in the years 1992-1996, the female MKs legislated in proportion to their representation in the Knesset: women constituted 9% of the Knesset, and they initiated and passed 9% of laws. However, during the next two terms, the legislative activity of the female MKs was double that of their statistical representation in the Knesset.

In the years 1996-1999, females were only 8% of MKs, but they were responsible for 15% of the laws in the Knesset (almost twice as many as their statistical representation). Then, in the years 1999-2003, 12% of the MKs were female, and they were responsible for the 24% of the legislation in the Knesset, i.e., literally double, or 200%, of their representation in the Knesset.

Summary and Conclusions

In this study, we have analyzed the factors which explain the remarkable increase in private legislation in Israel in the decade-and-a-half from 1992 to 2006, as well as the strategies which help private legislation succeed. This legislation has supreme significance in the democratic life of a country because the law serves as the keystone for determining the values, the culture, the norms, the proscriptions, and the prescriptions in the lives of individual citizens and the society as a whole.

Based on this study, it turns out that there are a number of factors which explain the significant growth of private legislation in Israel in the years 1999-2006. They are the following:

A. *Professionalism in managing legislation and the strategies and tactics of political negotiation*

- The professionalism of MKs in political bargaining—the acquisition and the development of skills, strategies, and tactics for managing the negotiation of legislation—significantly increased its scope. Four strategies have been found to be extremely important in the MKs' estimation: wisdom of compromise, the secret of stubbornness, skills in the procedural maneuvering of the agenda, and the timing of cultural and psychological aspects of negotiations.

- Other MKs, coalitions of interest groups, and the assistance of extra-parliamentary groups play a crucial role in promoting private legislation.

- The government has adapted to the new rules of the game and had used MKs' legislative initiatives to promote private interests (creating loyalty and stability). When the reality changed, the government revised the rules of the game and limited private legislation (2002).

B. *Contribution of ethical considerations and initiatives of MKs*

- Laws enacted at the initiative of MKs give a values-based, public response to issues that are important for the public but have been left unanswered by the government, so that an MK can throw his or her lot in with private legislative initiatives.

C. *Macro-political changes that strengthen private legislation*

- This change is expressed in the greater participation of MPs in the shaping of policy and their embracing the role of political initiators. (This process took place as the parties' dominance was fading and, in parallel, the legislature was weakened.)

101

- The macro-political, values-based, social changes in Israel in the 1990's and the transition to an "open society" swept through the political domain as well, reinterpreting the MK's role as more individualistic.

- A new balance was struck between the branches of government. The growing power of the executive branch (through the empowerment of the Economic Arrangements Law) and the growing power of the judiciary (with the expansion of judicial activism) pushed MKs to initiate more extensive legislative activity.

One hypothesis is that the change emerged from the implementation of primary elections amongst the major political parties (1992); the theory is that this caused private legislation to be viewed as a tool for realizing the aim of reelection. However, this has not been borne out by the research. In opposition to the research literature, this study has found no correlation between legislative accomplishments and reelection to the Knesset. In the research of Professor Tamir Shaefer (2001), focusing on the intersection of MKs' activity, the media, and the elections process, a similar finding was discovered.

Contributions of the present research

The present research is the first comprehensive study of the dramatic changes that have occurred with respect to the source of legislation in Israel: from the unchallenged role of the government in initiating legislation during the first 12 parliaments (1949-1992) to MKs assuming the lead role in this respect during the decade 1992-2003. There has been very little research thus far on the functioning of the Knesset in general and on private members' legislation in particular. This fact is particularly perturbing when one considers the extensive research literature that exists on Israel's legal system and the rulings of its courts. The present research should contribute to the following aspects of the academic literature:

1. **Theoretical contribution to the perception of the role of the legislator as political initiator in modern parliamentarianism.** Most of the research literature relates to the MK as a "team player" of his faction and his party. The conception and findings on the role of the legislator as independent political initiator and as responsible for policy formation build up to an important theoretical perspective. The research highlights the complexity of the parliamentary system in which the government, whose ministers are drawn from the political party leadership, has acquired increased power, in effect seizing from the Knesset the role of initiating legislation, while the role of the MKs has been reduced to ratifying that legislation.

2. **Study of the ideological motivation of the individual MK (and not only of the political parties) concomitant with motive of re-election.** Previous research into private legislation initiatives in Israel has focused primarily on the MK's motivation to seek re-election, the budgetary aspect, and the way in which such initiatives clash with the institution of government.

The present research concentrates more on the centrality of the ideological and value-based component of the motives for legislative initiatives. It further reveals the existence of ideologically-motivated organizations that form the basis and source of private legislation initiatives and lays the factual foundation for follow-up research on the important contribution of private legislation to the formation of social policies in Israel.

3. **Theoretical contribution to the analysis of legislative processes such as political negotiations (not only from the legal, procedural, and budgetary perspectives).** The research will contribute to characterizing and discerning the way decisions on legislation are made, such as political negotiations between MKs and the government, with the involvement of various interest groups. A contribution similar to the strategic and tactical analysis made by Wildavsky (1966, 1975) and Fenno (1966, 1973) in regard to budgetary procedures of the US House of Representatives is made by the present research vis-à-vis private legislation in Israel, using the theories and methods of negotiation strategy which were the prime tool of research in the field of political negotiation. Theories relating to labor relations between employer and employees contributed to an innovative understanding of the legislation process as a process of political negotiation between the initiating MK and the government, with the support of extra-parliamentary mediators.

4. **Innovative research into the comparative perspective of private legislation.** In the study comparing private legislation in Israel with that in several European parliaments, emphasis was placed on comparison between the laws that were passed, based on the assumption that the significant data relate to the draft bills actually passed into law (and not the number of draft bills that were tabled). The analysis of this aspect revealed that in the European parliaments studied as well, the percentage of legislation initiated by private Members of Parliament is far from negligible, fluctuating between just over 10%-35% of all legislation passed.

Conclusions

1. **There is a need to stress and highlight the very significant contribution of private legislative initiatives to shaping the society of the State of Israel.** The domain of private legislative initiatives and issues has had a far-reaching influence on the advancement of social and humanistic views in Israel, helping the weak populations in the country by reducing socio-economic gaps. It is essential to disseminate this in the public consciousness. Similarly, the research attests to the emphasis on values-based, ideological elements in the legislative initiative, confirming the assumption of Putnam (1973), that this approach has a not insignificant weight in the election, behavior, and political activity of each MK.

2. **The term "interest group" is exceedingly complex.** The study reveals that this generalization is flawed, unless there is an explicit distinction between **public** interest groups (even in the economic sphere), and the wealthy who have a **personal** economic interest. We see this in the mobilization to pass the Banking Law, the Fuel Law, the Electric Corporation Law, etc. Because of this issue, we need a different theoretical approach to interest groups and the tools which stand at the disposal of legislative houses to deal with them.

3. **Parliamentarians may need a training program.** In light of the centrality of initiatives and the importance of skills, strategies, and tactics in advancing private legislation, it may be necessary to devise training and preparation program for MKs. It appears that controlling information and skills is very helpful. Still, the question must be asked: can this be taught? Is it appropriate to train the parliamentarians not only to cultivate a general socio-political perspective, but also to use the secrets of professional political negotiation and the advancement of legislation? It may be that the same principles which are imparted and studied as the foundations of the academic, diplomatic, and business world must be taught in the political world as well.

4. **Cooperation is more desirable than confrontation.** The clear preference of all of the MKs is to adopt a general view of the "perceived feasibility model". This formulation suffices to influence the relationships between the authorities, preferring models of cooperation to confrontational models, even when huge political disagreements break out.

5. **Catalysts for government legislation**: From the interviews, it emerges that private legislation serves as a catalyst for the government to make laws and also contributes to the improvement and advancement of issues because of "legislative deterrence." By the MKs' estimation, there was no other idea that had the same effectiveness, whether it be proposals for discussion, queries, etc. No parliamentary tool in the MK's kit is as powerful in influencing the shaping of policy as the "whip" of proposing bills and the legislation itself.

6. **Stubbornness and determination are essential qualities for a parliamentarian.** These elements are integral for dealing with the great amount of work that legislation requires; the fact is that this process is a marathon, not a sprint; it is not a one-off media coup. In this regard, the differences between MKs become sharpened based on the form of their activity. The distinctions which arose from many interviews were that there are three types of activities by MKs: parliamentary activities, media activities, and interest-group activities. Further discussion and research into this system of classification may be worthwhile for investigating parliamentary activity.

7. **Legislation may be affected by gender.** This issue has only been partially investigated. It appears that just as in many other domains, the relationship between gender and legislation is

worth further study. Two question is particular remain: on the one hand, do women in parliament contribute an extra value in legislation; and on the other, is there importance in analyzing the existing legislation in different parliaments for equality between the sexes and its correlation with the advancement of women's status in those countries?

8. **Rhetoric has an important influence.** Here too the idea arises, just as it does when it comes to training to improve negotiating skills: can training in the art of rhetoric enhance the quality of the activity of MKs, including in the sphere of legislation?

9. **The cultural-psychological point of view is central in political bargaining.** Greater study of this topic is needed, as it stands more and more in the center of the dialogue amid the newest research in negotiation.

Finally, there are other issues which arose in the research, though they were not discussed in this book. We will point to three additional conclusions arising from the study.

10. **There is no correlation between legislative achievements and the odds of reelection.** This finding has far-reaching implications for the shaping of democracy, parliamentarism, and the role of the MK as an initiator of legislation. This finding disproves the theories raised in research literature, as well as the populist image which is affixed to the initiators of private legislation. If so, one may say with confidence that the initiators of legislation propose laws for substantive reasons, not for populist ones.

This finding already has had a great influence on the parliamentary activity of MKs, and it is likely to develop in a far-reaching way in terms of MKs' considerations in everything which touches on their order of priorities at work. One possibility is that MKs will isolate the factors which help reelection and adopt mainly forms of activity which strengthen their chances of reelection. Such a politically expedient conclusion, were it to be accepted, would not only be troubling; it would also be dangerous for the democratic regime and the ability to build and shape a rational, qualitative, and flourishing society.

A second possibility is that politicians will succeed in finding a way to integrate the desire for reelection with the desire for influential activity.

A third possibility is that if the second approach turns out to be unrealistic for a high percentage of MKs, there will be a need to reexamine the procedure of primary elections in the parties. A new direction, for example, might be devising integrated models lying between open elections and an organizing body. This seems to be at odds with the spirit of democratization which characterizes societies and political parties in the third millennium, but from a theoretical standpoint the disconnection between parliamentary activity and the chances of political survival justifies the continuation of the research and a public, theoretical rethinking of the methods of elections.

11. **There is a pressing need to rescind the limits on private legislation in Israel.** These limits were anchored in law in 2002, but the findings of the present research attest that the decision to place limits on private legislation has retarded and will continue to retard the socio-economic progress of the State of Israel. This problem justifies and obligates the total annulment of these limits. At the very least, they may be minimized, so that the allowed budgetary cost of a private bill would increase from NIS 5 million to NIS 30-50 million, and the majority required to authorize a private bill that the government opposes would decrease from fifty to thirty MKs.

12. **Canceling or minimizing the widespread use of the Economic Arrangements Law is essential.** Since 1985, this has been part of the Budget Law. The Economic Arrangements Law is a mechanism unique to the State of Israel, allowing the government to pass changes in budgetary policy in an antidemocratic way. This issue is the focus of great criticism, and it has even risen to the High Court of Justice, which did not spare it from its own condemnation. Despite this, the High Court left the Knesset the job of rescinding the law or minimizing its use. From the present research, it is clear that the Economic Arrangements Law has a negative impact on private legislation in the Knesset because it allows the government and the Knesset to delay the implementation of any law, even after it has been passed in a democratic way. It also undermines the notion of fair play in the negotiations between the MK as legislator and the government.

Bibliography

1992-2003, *Annual Knesset Statistics.*

Anderson, C.W. 1979, "Political Design and the Representation of Interests", in Schmitter, P.C. and Lehmbruch, G. (eds.), *Trends Toward Corporatist Intermediation*, Beverly Hills: Sage, 271-297.

Andeweg, R.B. 1996, "Elite-Mass Linkage in Europe: Legitimacy Crisis or Party Crisis", in J. Hayward (ed.), *Elitism, Populism, and European Politics*, Oxford: Clarendon Press, 232-233.

Andeweg, R.B. 1997. "Role Specialization or Role Switching? Dutch MPs between Electorate and Executive", in Muller, W.C. & Saalfeld, T. (eds.), 1997, *Members of Parliament in Western Europe: Roles and Behavior*, London: Frank Cass, p.110-127.

Arendt, H. 1973, *The Origins of Totalitarianism*, New York: Harcourt, Brace & Jovanovich.

Aristotle 1954, *Rhetoric*. Trans. W. Rhys Roberts. Oxford: Clarendon Press.

Barker, F. and Levine, S. 1999, "The Individual Parliamentary Member and International Change: The Changing Role of New Zealand Members of Parliament", *Journal of Legislative Studies* 5(3), 105-130.

Barnea, M.F. and Schwartz, S.H. 1998, "Values and Voting", *Political Psychology* 19(1), 17-40.

Barrett, E. J. 1997, "Gender and Race in the State House: The Legislative Experience." *Social Science Journal* 34(2), 131–144.

Ben-Arieh, A. 1999, *Influence of Members of the 13th Knesset on Welfare Policy*, Ph.D. dissertation, Jerusalem: Hebrew University.

Berkman, M. and O'Connor, R. 1993, "Do Women Legislators Matter: Female Legislators and State Abortion Policy", *American Politics Quarterly* 21(1), 102-124.

Birley, S. and MacMillan, I.C. (eds.) 1993, *International Perspective on Entrepreneurship Research*, London: Pergamion.

Boissevain, J. 1974, *Friends of Friends: Networks, Manipulators and Coalitions*, Oxford: B. Blackwell.

Brams S. J. and Taylor, A. 1996, *Fair Division*, New York: Cambridge University Press.

Brigg, M. 2003, "Mediation, Power, and Cultural Differences", *Conflict Resolution Quarterly* 20, 287-306.

Brockhaus, R.H. and Horwitz, P.S. 1985, "The Psychology of the Entrepreneur", in Sexton, D.L. and Smilor, R.W. (eds.), *The Art and Science of Entrepreneurship*, Cambridge, MA: Ballinger.

Bueno de Mesquita, B. 2003, *The Logic of Political Survival*, Cambridge, MA: MIT Press.

Chazan, N. 2005, "The Knesset", Israel Affairs 11(2), 392-416.

Checkel, J. 1997, Ideas and International Political Change: Soviet/Russian Behavior and the End of the Cold War, New Haven: Yale University Press.

Coleman, W.D. and Perl, A. 1999, "Internationalized Policy Environments and Policy Network Analysis", *Political Studies* XLVII, 691-709.

Copi, I. M. 1953, *Introduction to Logic*. New York: Macmillan.

Doring, H. 1995, "Is Government Control of the Agenda Likely to Keep Legislative Inflation` at Bay?", in Doring, H. (ed.), *Parliaments and Majority Rule in Western Europe*, Frankfurt: Campus Verlag, 654–687.

Doron, G. and Sened, I. 2001, *Political Bargaining: Theory, Practice, and Process*, London: Sage.

Dow, B. J. 2004, "Fixing Feminism: Women's. Liberation and the Rhetoric of Television Documentary", *Quarterly Journal of Speech* 90, 53-80.

Erickson, F. 1986, *Qualitative Methods* Vol. 2, N.Y: Macmillan Publishing

Fenno, R. F. 1966, *The Power of the Purse: Appropriations Politics in Congress*, Boston: Little, Brown and Company.

Fenno, R. F. 1973, *Congressmen in Committees*, Boston: Little, Brown and Company.

Fenno, R. F. 1978, *Home Style*, Boston: Little, Brown and Company.

Fiorina, A.M. and Rohde, W.D. 1989, *Home Style and Washington Work*, Ann Arbor: University of Michigan Press.

Fishbein, M. and Ajzen, I. 1975, *Beliefs Attitudes, Intention and Behavior, An Introduction to Theory and Research*, Massachusetts: Addison Wesley.

Galin, A. 1996, *The Dynamics of Negotiation - From Theory to Practice*, Tel Aviv University: Ramot.

Galin, A. 2005, *Negotiation - The Hidden Dimension*, Tel Aviv University: Ramot.

Gastil, R.D. 1990, "The Comparative Survey of Freedom: Experiences and Suggestions", *Studies in Cooperative International Development* 25, 25-50.

Goldberg, G. 2003, *Ben-Gurion against the Knesset*, London: Frank Cass.

Hall, A.P. 1993, "Policy Paradigms, Social Learning, and State, The Case of Economic Policymaking in Britain", *Comparative Politics* 25(2), 275-296.

Hansen, R. and King, D. 2001, "Eugenic Ideas, Political Interests, and Policy Variance: Immigration and Sterilization Policy in Britain and the US", *World Politics* 53(2), 237-262.

Hofstede, G. 1991, *Cultures and Organizations – Software of the Mind*, New YorK: HarperCollins.

Howlett, M. and Ramesh, M. 1995, *Studying Public Policy: Policy Cycles and Policy Subsystem*, Toronto: Oxford University Press.

ISEF 2002 Report on Parliamentary Activity, the International Sephardic Education Foundation.

Johnson, B.R. 1990, "Toward a Multidimensional of Entrepreneurship: The Case of Achievement Motivation and Entrepreneur", *Entrepreneurship: Theory and Practice* 14(2), 139-161.

Kamir, O. 2005, *Israeli Honor and Dignity: Social Norms, Gender Politics and the Law*, Jerusalem: Carmel (Hebrew).

Kamir, O. 2009, *Harassed – Living with the Israel's Sexual Harassment Law*, Tel Aviv: Hakibbutz Hameuchad and Carmel.

Kenny, W.L and Grothlushen, A.D. 1984, "Making the Case for Case Study", *Journal of Anthropology* 2, 53-74.

Key, V.O. 1964, *Politics, Parties and Pressure Groups*, New York, Crowell.

Kingdon, J.W. 1995, *Agendas, Alternatives and Public Policies*, New York: Harper Collins.

Kubler, Daniel 2001, "Understanding Policy Change with the Advocacy Coalition Framework: An Application to Swiss Drug Policy", *Journal of European Public Policy* 8 (4), 623–641.

Kurian, G.T. (ed.) 1998, *World Encyclopedia of Parliaments and Legislatures*, Washington D.C: Congressional Quarterly Inc.

Lebaron, M. J. and Zumeta, Z.D. 2003, "Windows on Diversity: Laws, Cultures and Mediation Practice", *Conflict Resolution Quarterly* 20, 467-472.

Leibes, T. 1999, "The Representation of the Public in the Media", *European Journal of Communication Research* 23, 321-329.

Lemish, D. 2000, "The Whore and the Other: Israeli Images of Female Immigrants from the Former USSR", *Gender and Society* 14(2), 333-349.

Lijphart, A. 1999, *Patterns of Democracy*, New-Haven: Yale University Press.

Longley, L.D and Hoffman, T.M. 1999, "Parliamentary Members and Leaders as Agents for Reform: Parliamentary and Regime Change Revisited", *Journal of Legislative Studies* (3), 131-208.

Loewenberg, G. 1972, "Comparative Legislative Research" in Patterson, S.C. and Wahlke J. C. (eds.), *Comparative Legislative Behavior: Frontiers of Research*, New York: Wiley-Inter Science.

Loewenberg, G. And Patterson, S.C. 1979, *Comparing Legislatures*, Boston: Little, Brown and Company.

Lutz, D.S. and James, R.W. 1976, *Coalitions in Legislatures: A Review of the Evidence*, Beverly Hills: Sage.

MacKinnon, C. 1979, *Sexual Harassment of Working Women: A Case of Sex Discrimination*, New Haven: Yale.

Maor, A. "The Dramatic Growth of Private Legislation in Israel: 1992-2003", *Israel Study Forum* 2008, 23, 84-103.

Maor, A. 2009, "Private Legislation as a Strategy of Political Negotiation", *Public Administration* 87(4), 750-761.

Maor, A., 2009, *Private Legislation of Knesset Members*, Tel Aviv: Hakibbutz Hameuchad.(Hebrew).

Maor, A. 2010, "How NGOs Help to Break Down Political Borders in Private Legislation in Parliaments", in Medina-Rivera, A. and Wilberschied, L. (eds), *Crossing Over*, Cleveland.

Marsh, D. and Read, M. 1988, *Private Members' Bills*, Cambridge: Cambridge University.

Mattson, I. 1995, "Private Members' Initiatives and Amendments", in Doring, H. (ed.), *Parliaments and Majority Rule in Western Europe*, Frankfurt: Campus Verlag, 448-487.

Maurer, L.M. 1999, "Parliamentary Influence in a New Democracy: The Spanish Congress", *The Journal of Legislative Studies* 5(2), 24-45.

Mayhew, R.D, 1974. *Congress- The Electoral Connection*, New Haven: Yale University Press.

McClleland, D.C. 1987, "Characteristics of Successful Entrepreneurs", *The Journal of Creative Behavior* 21(3), 219-233.

Mezey, M.L. 1979, *Comparative Legislatures*, Durham: Duke University Press.

Mezey, M.L. 1994, "New Perspectives on Parliamentary Systems: A Review Article", *Legislative Studies Quarterly* 19, 429-441.

Mill, J.S. 1946, *On Liberty and Considerations on Representative Government*, Oxford: Bazil Blackwell.

Milgrom, P. and Roberts, J. 1990, "Bargaining Costs, Influence Costs, and the Organization of Economic Activity", in Alt, J.E. and Shepsle, K.A. (eds.), *Perspective on Positive Political Economy*, Cambridge: Cambridge University Press.

Morris, M.H. 1998, *Entrepreneurial Intensity*, London: Quorum Books.

Muller, W.C. and Saalfeld, T. (eds.) 1997, *Members of Parliament in Western Europe: Roles and Behavior*, London: Frank Cass.

Mullins, J.W. and Cardozo, B.N. 1993, "New Ventures Strategies and Start-Up Environment: Concepts, Measurement, and Research Agenda", in Birley, S. and MacMillan I.C. (eds.), *International Perspective on Entrepreneurship Research*, London, North-Holland.

Nachmias, D. and Arbel-Ganz, O. 2003, "The Crisis of Governance: Government Service", in Cohen-Almagor, R., *Israeli Democracy at the Crossroad*, London: Frank-Cass.

Neckermann, P. J. 1991, *The Coalition Processes in the Federal Republic of Germany: A Study of the Influence of Political Leaders on the Process of Coalition Building*, Ann Arbor: University Microfilms International.

Newman, B. and Sheth, J. 1987, *A Theory of Political Choice Behavior*, Praeger: New York

Nisbet, R.A. 1966, *The Sociological Tradition*, New York: Basic Books.

Nagel, S. 2002, *Creativity and Government*, New York: Nova Science Publishers.

Norton, P. and Wood, D. 1990, "Constituency Service by Members of Parliament: Does it Contribute to Personal Vote", *Parliamentary Affairs* 35(1), 59-72.

Norton, P. 1993, *Does Parliament Matter?* New York: Harvester Wheatsheaf.

Norton, P. 1997, in: Muller, W.C. and Saalfeld, T. (eds.), *Members of Parliament in Western Europe: Roles and Behavior*, London: Frank Cass, 17-31.

Norton, P. 1998, "Old Institution, New Institutionalism? Parliament and Government in the UK", in Norton, P. (ed.), *Parliaments and Governments in Western Europe*, London

Norton, P. 1999, "Introduction", in Norton, P. (ed.), *Parliaments and Pressure Groups in Western Europe*, London: Frank Cass, 1–18.

Olson, D.M. 1994, *Democratic Legislative Institution*, New-York: M.E. Sharpe, 132-144.

Perelman, C. and Olbrechts-Tyteca, L. 1991, *The New Rhetoric: A Treatise on Argumentation*. South Bend: Notre Dame.

Pruitt, D. and Rubin, G. 1986, *Social Conflict*, New York: McGraw-Hill.

Putnam, D.R. 1973, *The Beliefs of Politicians*, New Haven: Yale University Press.

Radaelli, C.M. 1995, "The Role of Knowledge in the Policy Process", *Journal of European Public Policy*, 159-183.

Rawls, J. 1973, *The Liberal Theory of Justice: a Critical Examination of the Principal Doctrines in a Theory of Justice*, Oxford: Clarindon Press.

Richard, T.B. 2002, "Private Bills: A Theoretical and Empirical Study of Lobbying", *Public Choice* 111(1-2), p. 19.

Robinson, J. 1967, "Review of the Power of the Purse", *American Political Review* 51, 764-766.

Rokeach, M. 1973, *The Nature of Human Values*, New York: The Free Press.

Rothenberg, L.S. 1992, *Linking Citizens to Government: Interest Groups as Common Cause*, New York: Cambridge University Press.

Routledge, W.V. 1996, *The Government and Politics of France*

Rush, M. 1990, "Lobbying Parliament", *Parliamentary Affairs* 43(1), 141-148.

Sabatier, P. and Jenkins-Smith, H.C. (eds.) 1993, *Policy Change and Learning: An Advocacy Coalition Approach*, Boulder: Westview Press.

Schelling, T.C. 1963, *The Strategy of Conflict*, New York: Oxford University Press.

Schneider, A. and Ingram, H. 1990, "Behavioral Assumptions of Policy Tools", *Journal of Politics* 52(2).

Scott, R. and Herbenar, R J. 1979, *Parties in Crisis*, Utah: John Wiley and Sons.

Searing, D.D. 1994, *Westminster's World*, Cambridge, MA: Harvard University Press

Smith, R.A. 1995, "Interest Group Influence in the U.S. Congress, *Legislature Studies Quarterly* (20), 89-139.

Stake, R.E. 1978, "The Case Study Methods in Social Inquiry", *Educational Research* 7(2), 8.

Stevans, C.M. 1963, *Strategy and Collective Bargaining*, New York: McGraw-Hill.

Stone, D.A. (1989). "Causal Stories and the Formation of Policy Agendas", *Political Science Quarterly* 104(2), 281-301.

Strom, K. 1990, *Minority Government and Majority Rule*, New York: Cambridge University Press.

Surel, Y. 2000, "The Role of Cognitive and Normative Frames in Policy Making", *Journal of European Public Policy*, 7:4, 495-512.

Tarrow S.G. 2005, *The New Transnational Activism*, New York: Cambridge University Press.

Trocsanyi, L. 1996, "The Rights of the Legislative Initiative", *Seminar on the Democratic Functioning of Parliaments, Council of Europe*, 73-84.

Troper, M. 1992, "The Development of the Notion of Separation of Powers", *Israel Law Review*.

Van Waarden, F. 1992, "Dimensions and Types of Policy Networks", *European Journal of Political Research* 21, 29–52.

Vega, A. and Firestone, J. M. 1995, "The Effects of Gender on Congressional Behavior and the Substantive Representation of Women", *Legislative Studies Quarterly*, 213-222.

Walsh, J.I. 2000, "When do Ideas Matter? Explaining the Successes and Failures of Thatcherism Ideas (in the UK)", *Comparative Political Studies* 33 (4)**,** 483-516.

Wildavsky, A. 1964, *The Politics of the Budgetary*, Boston: Little, Brown.

Wildavsky A. 1975, *A Comparative Theory of Budgetary Processes*, Boston: Little Brown.

Wilke Henk, A.M. (ed) 1985, *Coalition Formation***,** Amsterdam : Netherlands.

Wright, M. 1956, *The Power Elite*, New York: Oxford University Press.

Yishai, Y. 1997, "Legislators and Interest Groups: Some Observations on the Israeli Scene", *The Journal of Legislative Studies* 3(2), 89-111.

VDM publishing house ltd.

Scientific Publishing House

offers

free of charge publication

of current academic research papers, Bachelor´s Theses, Master's Theses, Dissertations or Scientific Monographs

If you have written a thesis which satisfies high content as well as formal demands, and you are interested in a remunerated publication of your work, please send an e-mail with some initial information about yourself and your work to *info@vdm-publishing-house.com*.

Our editorial office will get in touch with you shortly.

VDM Publishing House Ltd.
Meldrum Court 17.
Beau Bassin
Mauritius
www.vdm-publishing-house.com

Made in the USA
San Bernardino, CA
06 November 2012